Complete Study Edition

Romeo & Juliet

Commentary | Complete Text | Glossary

edited by

SIDNEY LAMB

Associate Professor of English,
Sir George Williams University, Montreal

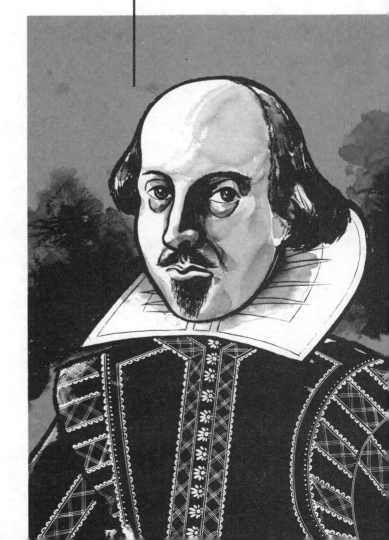

Cliff's Notes

INCORPORATED

LINCOLN, NEBRASKA   68501

ISBN 0-8220-1438-6

Romeo & Juliet

SHAKESPEARE WAS NEVER MORE MEANINGFUL—

. . . than when read in Cliff's "Complete Study Edition." The introductory sections give you all of the background information about the author and his work necessary for reading with understanding and appreciation. A descriptive bibliography provides guidance in the selection of works for further study. The inviting three-column arrangement of the complete text offers the maximum in convenience to the reader. Adjacent to the text there is a running commentary that provides clear supplementary discussion of the play as it develops. Obscure words and obsolete usages used by Shakespeare are explained in the glosses directly opposite to the line in which they occur. The numerous allusions are also clarified.

SIDNEY LAMB—

. . . the editor of this Shakespeare "Complete Study Edition," attended Andover Academy and Columbia University, receiving the Prince of Wales Medal for Philosophy and the Moyes Travelling Fellowship. Following graduate studies in Elizabethan literature at King's College, Cambridge, from 1949 to 1952, he became a member of the English Faculty of the University of London's University of the Gold Coast in West Africa. Professor Lamb joined the faculty of Sir George Williams University, Montreal, in 1956.

Romeo & Juliet

contents

hath bene fundry times publiquely :
right Honoyrable the Lord Cham
his Seruants.

THE MOST EX-
cellent and lamentable
Tragedie, of Romeo
and *Iuliet.*

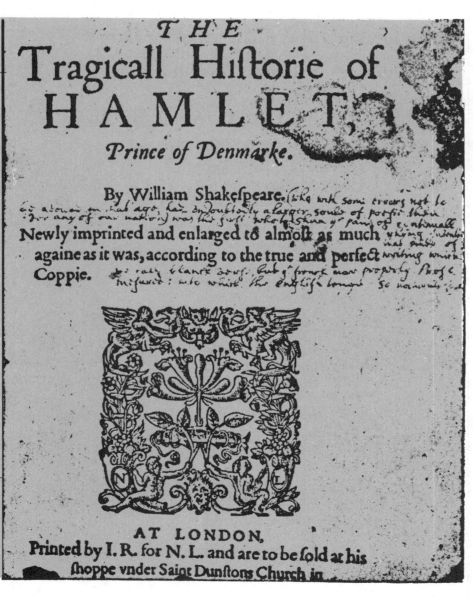

THE
Tragicall Hiſtorie of
HAMLET,
Prince of Denmarke.

By William Shakeſpeare.

Newly imprinted and enlarged to almoſt as much
againe as it was, according to the true and perfect
Coppie.

AT LONDON,
Printed by I. R. for N. L. and are to be ſold at his
ſhoppe vnder Saint Dunſtons Church in

Two books are essential to the library of any English-speaking household; one of these is the Bible and the other is the works of William Shakespeare. These books form part of the house furnishings, not as reading material generally, but as the symbols of religion and culture—sort of a twentieth-century counterpart of the ancient Roman household gods. This symbolic status has done a great deal of damage both to religion and to Shakespeare.

Whatever Shakespeare may have been, he was not a deity. He was a writer of popular plays, who made a good living, bought a farm in the country, and retired at the age of about forty-five to enjoy his profits as a gentleman. The difference between Shakespeare and the other popular playwrights of his time was that he wrote better plays —plays that had such strong artistic value that they have been popular ever since. Indeed, even today, if Shakespeare could col-

William to Shakespeare.

lect his royalties, he would be among the most prosperous of playwrights.

During the eighteenth century but mostly in the nineteenth, Shakespeare's works became "immortal classics," and the cult of Shakespeare-worship was inaugurated. The plays were largely removed from their proper place on the stage into the library where they became works of literature rather than drama and were regarded as long poems, attracting all the artistic and psuedo-artistic atmosphere surrounding poetry. In the nineteenth century this attitude was friendly but later, and especially in the early twentieth century, a strange feeling arose in the English-speaking world that poetry was sissy stuff, not for men but for "pansies" and women's clubs. This of course is sheer nonsense.

This outline will present a detailed analysis of the play and background information which will show the play in its proper perspective. This means seeing the play in relation to the other plays, to the history of the times when they were written, and in relation to the theatrical technique required for their successful performance.

G. B. Harrison's book *Introducing Shakespeare,* published by Penguin Books, will be of value for general information about Shakespeare and his plays. For reference material on the Elizabethan Theater, consult E. K. Chambers, *The Elizabethan Theatre* (four volumes). For study of the organization and production methods of this theater see *Henslowe's Diary* edited by W. W. Greg. Again for general reading the student will enjoy Margaret Webster's *Shakespeare Without Tears,* published by Whittlesey House (McGraw-Hill) in 1942.

The remainder of the Introduction will be divided into sections discussing Shakespeare's life, his plays, and his theater.

LIFE OF WILLIAM SHAKESPEARE

From the standpoint of one whose main interest lies with the plays themselves, knowledge of Shakespeare's life is not very important. Inasmuch as it treats of the period between 1592 and 1611, when the plays were being written, knowledge of his life is useful in that it may give some clues as to the topical matters introduced into the plays. For instance, the scene of Hamlet's advice to the players (Act III Scene ii) takes on an added significance when considered along with the fame and bombastic style of Edward Alleyn, the then famous actor-manager of the Lord Admiral's Players (the most powerful rivals of Shakespeare's company).

This biography is pieced together from the surviving public records of the day, from contemporary references in print, and from the London Stationer's Register. It is by no means complete. The skeletal nature of the biographical material available to scholars has led commentators in the past to invent part of the story to fill it out. These parts have frequently been invented by men who were more interested in upholding a private theory than in telling the truth, and this habit of romancing has led to a tradition of inaccurate Shakespearian biography. For this reason this outline may be of use in disposing of bad traditions.

In the heyday of the self-made man, the story developed that Shakespeare was a poor boy from the village, virtually uneducated, who fled from Stratford to London to escape prosecution for poaching on the lands of Sir Thomas Lucy, and there by his talent and a commendable industry raised himself to greatness. This rags-to-riches romance was in the best Horatio Alger tradition but was emphatically not true. The town records of Stratford make it clear that John Shakespeare, father of the playwright, was far from a pauper. He was a wealthy and responsible citizen who held in turn several municipal offices. He married (1557) Mary Arden, the daughter of a distinguished Catholic family. William, their third son, was baptized in the Parish Church in 1564. He had a good grammar school education. Ben Jonson's remark that Shakespeare had "small Latin and less Greek" did not mean the same in those days, when the educated man had a fluent command of

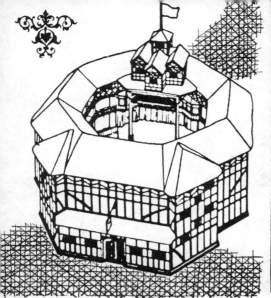

Exterior view of "The Globe"

Shakespeare's London

Interior view of "The Globe"

an introduction to Shakespeare

Latin and probably at least a reading knowledge of Greek, as it does now when classical scholars are few. The remark has been construed by the Horatio Alger people as meaning that Shakespeare reached London a semiliterate bumpkin; it is nonsense. It means merely that Shakespeare was not a university man, as most of the writers were, and that the University Wits were taking out their jealousy in snobbery and pointing out that Shakespeare used less purely literary symbolism than they did.

Shakespeare married Ann Hathaway when he was eighteen years old. She was some years older than he and the marriage seems to have been a rather hasty affair. Five months after the marriage, Suzanna, the first child, was born. Two years later, in 1585, twins Hamnet and Judith were baptized.

No one knows when Shakespeare came to London. The first mention of him occurs in the bad-tempered pamphlet which Robert Greene, one of the University Wits and a famous playwright, wrote just before his death. Greene complains of "an upstart crow, beautified with our feathers, that with his tiger's heart wrapped in a player's hide, supposes he is as well able to bombast out a blank verse as the best of you; and being an absolute Yohannes factotum, is in his own conceit the only Shakescene in a country." This was written in 1592 and indicates not only that Shakespeare was in

London at the time, but that he was writing plays and beginning to make such a name for himself as to call forth the jealous apprehension of an established writer.

The next year, 1593, was a year of plague, and by order of the Lord Mayor and the Aldermen, the theaters were closed. The players, disorganized by this action, went on tour outside of London. During this year Shakespeare's two long poems, *Venus and Adonis* and *The Rape of Lucrece,* were entered in the Stationer's Register. Both were dedicated to the Earl of Southampton.

The public theaters had not been established very long. The first of these, called the Theatre, was built for James Burbage in 1576. By 1594, there were three such theaters in London, the two new houses being the Curtain and the Rose. By 1594, also, the three most celebrated of the writers, Kyd, Greene, and Marlowe were dead, and Shakespeare had already a considerable reputation. Before this date the theaters had been largely low class entertainment and the plays had been of rather poor quality. Through the revival of classical drama in the schools (comedies) and the Inns of Court (tragedies), an interest had been created in the stage. The noblemen of the time were beginning to attend the public theaters, and their tastes demanded a better class of play.

Against the background of this

FLUVIUS

South 3 warke

increasing status and upper-class popularity of the theaters, Shakespeare's company was formed. After the 1594 productions under Alleyn, this group of actors divided. Alleyn formed a company called the Lord Admiral's Company which played in Henslowe's Rose Theatre. Under the leadership of the Burbages (James was the owner of the Theatre and his son Richard was a young tragic actor of great promise), Will Kemp (the famous comedian), and William Shakespeare, the Lord Chamberlain's company came into being. This company continued throughout Shakespeare's career. It was renamed in 1603, shortly after Queen Elizabeth's death, becoming the King's players.

The company played at the Theatre until Burbage's lease on the land ran out. The landlord was not willing to come to satisfactory terms. The company moved across the river and built the new Globe theater. The principal sharers in the new place were Richard and Cuthbert Burbage each with two and a half shares and William Shakespeare, John Heminge, Angustus Phillips, Thomas Pope, and Will Kemp, each with one share.

Burbage had wanted to establish a private theater and had rented the refectory of the old Blackfriars' monastery. Not being allowed to use this building he leased it to a man called Evans who obtained permission to produce plays acted by chil-

dren. This venture was so successful as to make keen competition for the existing companies. This vogue of child actors is referred to in *Hamlet,* Act II Scene ii.

The children continued to play at Blackfriars until, in 1608, their license was suspended because of the seditious nature of one of their productions. By this time the public attitude towards the theaters had changed, and Burbage's Company, now the King's players, could move into the Blackfriars theater.

Partners with the Burbages in this enterprise were Shakespeare, Heminge, Condell, Sly, and Evans. This was an indoor theater, whereas the Globe had been outdoors. The stage conditions were thus radically altered. More scenery could be used; lighting effects were possible. Shakespeare's works written for this theater show the influence of change in conditions.

To return to the family affairs of the Shakespeares, records show that in 1596 John Shakespeare was granted a coat of arms and, along with his son, was entitled to call himself "gentleman." In this year also, William Shakespeare's son Hamnet died. In 1597 William Shakespeare bought from William Underwood a sizable estate at Stratford, called New Place.

Shakespeare's father died in 1601, his mother, in 1608. Both of his daughters married, one in 1607, the other in 1616.

During this time, Shakespeare

went on acquiring property in Stratford. He retired to New Place probably around 1610 although this date is not definitely established, and his career as a dramatist was practically at an end. *The Tempest,* his last complete play, was written around the year 1611.

The famous will, in which he left his second best bed to his wife, was executed in 1616 and later on in that same year he was buried.

THE PLAYS

Thirty-seven plays are customarily included in the works of William Shakespeare. Scholars have been at great pains to establish the order in which these plays were written. The most important sources of information for this study are the various records of performances which exist, the printed editions which came out during Shakespeare's career, and such unmistakable references to current events as may crop up in the plays. The effect of the information gathered in this way is generally to establish two dates between which a given play must have been written. In *Hamlet* for instance, there is a scene in which Hamlet refers to the severe competition given to the adult actors by the vogue for children's performances. This vogue first became a serious threat to the professional companies in about 1600. In 1603 a very bad edition was published, without authorization, of *The*

Queen Elizabeth

an introduction
to Shakespeare

Elizabethan types

Lute, standing cup, stoop

Tragical History of Hamlet, Prince of Denmark by William Shakespeare. These two facts indicate that *Hamlet* was written between the years of 1600 and 1603. This process fixed the order in which most of the plays were written. Those others of which no satisfactory record could be found were inserted in their logical place in the series according to the noticeable development of Shakespeare's style. In these various ways we have arrived at the following chronological listing of the plays.

1591   *Henry VI Part I*
      Henry VI Part II
      Henry VI Part III
      Richard III
      Titus Andronicus
      Love's Labour Lost
      The Two Gentlemen
        of Verona
      The Comedy of Errors
      The Taming of the Shrew

1594   *Romeo and Juliet*
      A Midsummer Night's
        Dream
      Richard II
      King John
      The Merchant of Venice

1597   *Henry IV Part I*
      Henry IV Part II
      Much Ado About Nothing
      Merry Wives of Windsor
      As You Like It
      Julius Caesar
      Henry V
      Troilus and Cressida

1601   *Hamlet*
      Twelfth Night
      Measure for Measure
      All's Well That Ends Well

      Othello

1606   *King Lear*
      Macbeth
      Timon of Athens
      Antony and Cleopatra
      Coriolanus

1609   *Pericles*

1611   *Cymbeline*
      The Winter's Tale
      The Tempest
      Henry VIII

At this point it is pertinent to review the tradition of dramatic form that had been established before Shakespeare began writing. Drama in England sprang at the outset from the miracle and morality plays of the medieval guilds. These dramatized Bible stories became increasingly less religious as time passed until finally they fell into disrepute. The next development was the writing of so-called *interludes*. These varied in character but often took the form of bawdy farce. As the renaissance gathered force in England, Roman drama began to be revived at the schools and the Inns of Court. Before long English writers were borrowing plots and conventions wholesale from the classic drama. The Italian model was the most fashionable and consequently was largely adopted, but many features of the old *interludes* still persisted, especially in plays written for the public theaters.

With the development among the nobility of a taste for the theater, a higher quality of work became in demand. Very few of

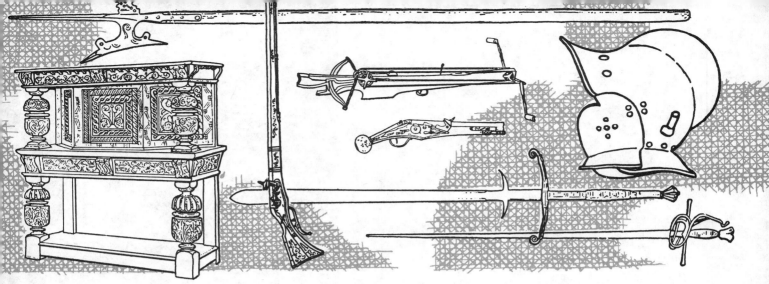

Court cupboard, crossbow, guns, sword, rapier, halberd, burgonet

the very early plays have survived. The reason for this is that the plays were not printed to be read; no one considered them worth the trouble. A play was strung together out of a set of stock characters and situations with frantic haste, often by as many as a dozen different men. These men who worked on plays did not regard their writing activity as of prime importance. They were primarily actors. With the cultivation of taste for better plays came the idea that the work of a playwright was an effort demanding special skill. The highborn audiences were interested in the plays themselves and began to include editions of their favorite plays in their libraries. With this demand for printed copies of the plays, the conception began of the dramatist as an artist in his own right, whether or not he acted himself (as most of them did).

By 1592, when Shakespeare began to make his personal reputation, a set of traditions had developed. This body of traditions gave Shakespeare the basic materials with which to work.

A special type of comedy writing had developed, centered around the name of John Lyly, designed for the sophisticated audience of the court and presented with lavish dances and decorative effects. This type of play was characterized by a delicately patterned artificiality of speech. The dialogue was studded with complicated references to Latin and Italian literature that the renaissance had made fashionable.

Shakespeare used this method extensively. In the early plays (before *The Merchant of Venice*) he was experimenting and wrote much that is nothing more than conventional. Later on, as his mature style developed, the writing becomes integral with and indispensable to the play and no longer appears artificial. In *Romeo and Juliet,* an early play, the following lines are spoken by Lady Capulet in urging Juliet to accept the Count Paris for her husband. These lines are brilliant but artificial, and the play seems to pause in order that this trick bit of word-acrobatics may be spoken.

Read o'er the volume of young
    Paris' face,
And find delight, writ there
    with beauty's pen.
Examine every married linea-
    ment,
And see how one another lends
    content:
And what obscured in this fair
    volume lies,
Find written in the margent of
    his eyes.
This precious book of love, this
    unbound lover,
To beautify him only needs a
    cover!

The other most important dramatic tradition was that of tragedy. The Elizabethan audiences liked spectacular scenes; they also had a great relish for scenes of sheer horror. This led to a school of tragic writing made popular by Kyd and Marlowe.

These plays were full of action and color and incredible wickedness, and the stage literally ran with artificial blood. Shakespeare's early tragedies are directly in this tradition, but later the convention becomes altered and improved in practice, just as that of comedy had done. The scene in *King Lear* where Gloucester has his eyes torn out stems from this convention. Lear, however, is a comparatively late play and the introduction of this scene does not distort or interrupt its organization.

Shakespeare's stylistic development falls into a quite well-defined progression. At first he wrote plays according to the habit of his rivals. He very quickly began experimenting with his technique. His main concern seems to be with tricks of language. He was finding out just what he could do. These early plays use a great deal of rhyme, seemingly just because Shakespeare liked writing rhyme. Later on, rhyme is used only when there is a quite definite dramatic purpose to justify it. Between the early plays and those which may be called mature (*The Merchant of Venice* is the first of the mature plays), there is a basic change in method. In the early works Shakespeare was taking his patterns from previous plays and writing his own pieces, quite consciously incorporating one device here and another there.

In the later period these tricks of the trade had been tested and

The world as known in 1600

Elizabethan coins

absorbed; they had become not contrived methods but part of Shakespeare's mind. This meant that, quite unconsciously, while his total attention was focused on the emotional and intellectual business of writing a masterpiece, he wrote in terms of the traditional habits he had learned and used in the earlier period. (*Henry IV*, *Julius Caesar*, *Henry V*, and *Hamlet* are the plays of this advanced stage.)

The group of plays between 1606 and 1609 shows a further new development. Having reached mastery of his medium in terms of dramatic technique (with *Othello*) and of power over the tension of thought in moving easily through scenes of comedy, pathos, and tragedy, he turned again to the actual literary quality of his plays and began to enlarge his scope quite beyond and apart from the theatrical traditions of his day. The early results of this new attempt are the two plays *King Lear* and *Macbeth*. The change in these plays is in the direction of concentration of thought. The attempt is, by using masses of images piled one on another, to convey shadings and intensities of emotion not before possible. He was trying to express the inexpressible. For example the following is from the last part of

an introduction
to Shakespeare

Lady Macbeth's famous speech in Act I, Scene v:

>   Come, thick night,
> And pall thee in the dunnest smoke of hell,
> That my keen knife see not the wound it makes,
> Nor heaven peep through the blanket of the dark,
> To cry, hold, hold!

Compare the concentrated imagery of this speech with Hamlet's soliloquy at the end of Act III, Scene ii.

> 'Tis now the very witching time of night,
> When churchyards yawn, and hell itself breathes out
> Contagion to this world: now could I drink hot blood,
> And do such bitterness as the day
> Would quake to look on.

The sentiment of these two speeches is similar, but the difference in method is striking and produces a difference again in the type of effect. The *Lear-Macbeth* type of writing produces a higher tension of subtlety but tends to collect in masses rather than to move in lines as the lighter, more transparent writing of *Hamlet* does.

Shakespeare's last plays were conceived for the new indoor theater at Blackfriars and show this is in a more sophisticated type of staging. In *The Tempest*, last and most celebrated of these late comedies, there is dancing, and much complicated staging (such as the disappearing banquet, the ship at sea, and so on). The writing of plays for the

more distinguished audience of Blackfriars, and the increased stage resources there provided, influenced the form of the plays.

The writing of these plays forms a culmination. In his early apprenticeship Shakespeare had been extravagant in word-acrobatics, testing the limits of his technique. In the Lear-Macbeth period of innovation he had tried the limits of concentrated emotion to the point almost of weakening the dramatic effectiveness of the plays. In *The Tempest* his lines are shaken out into motion again. He seems to have been able to achieve the subtlety he was after in verse of light texture and easy movement, no longer showing the tendency to heaviness or opacity visible in *King Lear* and *Macbeth*.

THE THEATER

The first public theater in London was built in the year 1576 for James Burbage and was called simply The Theatre. Before this time players' companies had performed for the public in the courtyards of the city inns. For a more select public they frequently played in the great halls of institutions, notably the Inns of Court. The stage and auditorium of the Elizabethan theater were based on these traditions and combined features of both the hall and the inn-yard. The auditorium was small. There was a pit where the orchestra seats would be in a modern playhouse; this section was for the lowest classes who stood during the performances. Around the

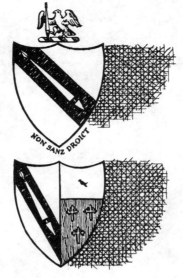

Shakespeare's Coat of Arms

Wood cut camp illustration

wall was a gallery for the gentry. The galleries and the tiring-house behind the fore-stage were roofed; the rest was open to the sky. The stage consisted of a very large platform that jutted out so that the pit audience stood on three sides of it. Behind this, under the continuation behind the stage of the gallery, was the inner stage; this was supplied with a curtain, but the open fore-stage was not. Above this inner stage was a balcony (really a continuation of the gallery), forming still another curtained stage. This gallery was used for kings addressing subjects from balconies, for the storming of walls, for Juliet's balcony and bedroom, for Cleopatra's monument and so on. Costumes and properties were extravagant (such as guillotines, fountains, ladders, etc.); extensive music was constantly used and such sound effects as cannon, drums, or unearthly screams were common; but there was no painted scenery as we know it; there was no darkness to focus attention on the stage, no facilities for stage-lighting. All these things are in marked contrast to the modern stage conventions and thus a serious problem of adaptation is posed when it comes to producing the plays under present day conditions.

The advantages are not all with the modern stage. It is true that the modern or picture stage can do more in the way of realistic effects, but this kind of realism is not important to good

drama. In fact there has been a recent trend away from realistic scenery in the theater back to a conventional or stylized simplicity.

One effect of Shakespeare's stage upon his work was to make the scenes in the plays more person-scenes than place-scenes. As a matter of fact in many cases the places assigned in the texts to various scenes were not in the original and have only been added by an editor who did not understand this very fact.

It used to be said that *Antony and Cleopatra* could not be staged and was written to be read rather than acted. The grounds for this statement were that in the fourth act there were no less than fourteen scenes. To some, a scene means a change of place and requires a break in the play while scenery is shifted. To Shakespeare these scenes meant no such thing; they meant, simply, that there were fourteen different groupings of people, successively and without any break, carrying on the action of the play. The scene headings when added should have been (1) Caesar, (2) Antony and Cleopatra, (3) the common soldiers, etc., instead of (1) Before Alexandria, (2) Alexandria, a room in the palace, etc. By this you may see that with all its limitations, the Elizabethan stage had a measure of flexibility that the modern stage could envy.

Fashions in staging Shakespeare have altered radically in the last few years. At the close

of the nineteenth century, Sir Herbert Beerbohm Tree staged a spectacular series of pageant productions. All the tricks of romantic realistic staging were used and, if necessary, the play was twisted, battered, and re-written to accommodate the paraphernalia.

The modern method is to produce the plays as nearly according to the text as possible and work out a compromise to achieve the sense of space and of flexibility necessary, yet without departing so far from the stage habits of today as to confuse or divert the audience. This technique was inaugurated by Granville-Barker in the early twentieth century. With the exception of such extravagant stunts as Orson Welles' production of *Julius Caesar* in modern dress (set in Chicago and complete with tommy-guns), the prevailing practice now is to use simple, stylized scenery adapted to the needs of producing the play at full length.

Much can be done in the way of learning Shakespeare through books, but the only sure way is to see a well produced performance by a good company of actors. Whatever genius Shakespeare may have possessed as a psychologist, philosopher, or poet, he was first of all a man of the theater, who knew it from the inside, and who wrote plays so well-plotted for performance that from his day up to the present, no great actor has been able to resist them.

❧ an introduction to

SOURCE OF PLOT

Shakespeare borrowed the plot from Arthur Brooke's long poem *The Tragicall Hystory of Romeus and Juliet* (1562), an Italian story which Brooke found in a French translation by Boisteau. It is probable that Shakespeare also read a prose version of Boisteau's story by William Painter (*The goodly History of the true and constant love betweene Romeo and Julietta*) in the second volume of his *Palace of Pleasure* (1567). There was, too, a play on the story (since lost) which Brooke mentions in his Preface *To the Reader* ("the same argument lately set forth on stage") and Shakespeare may have seen it. This is only guess-work, however, and it has to be remembered that for Shakespeare to be familiar with it, the play to which Brooke refers must have kept the stage for at least twenty years.

Time and time again Shakespeare built great works of art out of the well-known stories of his day, which only seem "Shakespearean" to us because we do not know his minor contemporaries.

What is more important is Shakespeare's treatment of the plot. As usual he took somebody else's story and gave it new life and new beauty. But since he follows Brooke's poem very closely, his divergences therefrom have all the more significance. They were evidently deliberate. For the sake of convenience his chief alterations are put under separate headings.

COMPRESSION OF TIME

Shakespeare compresses the nine months' action of Brooke's poem into less than five days, in the interests of swiftness, power and unity of action.

The movement of the play is clearly marked, according to the following time-table:

SUNDAY: The Play opens with a street brawl at nine o'clock in the morning. Romeo and Juliet first meet at a party the same night. After the party Romeo gets into Capulet's garden and from the ground talks to Juliet at her window.

MONDAY: They are married in the afternoon. Thereafter Romeo kills Tybalt and is banished, but he defies the law to spend the night with Juliet. Late that night old Capulet arranges Juliet's marriage with Paris Thursday morning.

TUESDAY: As dawn breaks Romeo leaves Juliet. He has no sooner gone than Juliet is told by her parents that she is to marry Paris, and in despair she goes to Friar Laurence's cell.

Late that night the wedding is advanced to take place the next morning.

Before she goes to sleep Juliet

10

The Tragedy of Romeo & Juliet

takes the Friar's draught.

WEDNESDAY: At early dawn Juliet is discovered "dead", and is taken to the family tomb late in the day.

THURSDAY: Romeo hears of Juliet's death and buys poison.

FRIDAY: During the very early morning, while it is still dark, Romeo comes to the tomb, and the rest of the play takes place before full dawn.

The student will probably get a surprise when he sees this time-table set out, for although swift when its time is analyzed, the play is not so swift in its general impression. Juliet tells Romeo that their love is "too rash, too unadvised, too sudden" and

This bud of love, by summer's ripening breath,
May prove a beauteous flower when next we meet.

When they next day meet, therefore, the audience has the impression that there has been a delay, but the delay, in fact, is only a matter of hours. The Nurse tells Romeo that she angers Juliet "sometimes" and tells her "that Paris is the properer man"; she speaks as if she has known Romeo a long time, and, according to Juliet, has praised him "above compare so many thousand times," yet, in fact, she has known him for only a couple of days. It seems as if Romeo has been banished longer than a day when he has had time to take

such note of shops and shopkeepers round about. Above all, the growth of the character of Juliet from girl to woman has the strongest effect in lengthening the time-sense. And at the end, after being crossed in love for four days, Romeo talks of "this world-wearied flesh."

DEVELOPMENT OF CHARACTERS

It would be a mistake to think that the borrowing of the outline of the story in any way detracts from Shakespeare's genius. The plot is the least important part of a play. Shakespeare's great artistic power is in characterization. A story with a "realistic" plot has no life if the characters are wooden, but a crude plot becomes alive when living people inform it. Shakespeare was often very careless in his plots; it is in his use of the plot that he shows his imagination.

The plot of Romeo and Juliet is no exception. It is very thin at its central point, and the amount of coincidence is incredible. Apart from the use of a drug producing a death that is not death, it is unnatural that when Juliet is found "dead" in bed none of the household should suspect suicide, that no one should want to find out the cause of her death, and that no one should see the empty vial

and the dagger by her side. (Shakespeare appears to have forgotten these.) But things like this have little weight. *Romeo and Juliet* is one of the world's greatest plays because Romeo and Juliet are what Shakespeare has made them.

Shakespeare takes two years off Juliet's age. According to Brooke, "Scarce saw she yet full sixteen years." It may seem to many that an older girl would have been more credible. Presumably the alteration was to throw into relief her development from an obedient girl to a self-assured heroine — the younger she is to begin with the more noticeable is the fullness of her character at the end. It should be remembered also that on Shakespeare's stage the part would be acted by a boy of about this age.

Two important people developed by Shakespeare from mere names into characters of his own are Mercutio and the Nurse. They are both outside the main line of progress of the play, but have a bustling vitality in their own right. They are introduced for contrast — Mercutio with Romeo, and the Nurse with Juliet—and also for wit and comic relief.

Tybalt is another character developed by Shakespeare, and again the dramatic reason is the same, for contrast with Romeo.

The events of Shakespeare's plays depend on the characters of the people in them, not on an arbitrary fate: it was the nature of Mercutio and Tybalt which caused Romeo's banishment.

CONSTRUCTION

There is, in *Romeo and Juliet,* no sub-plot. The construction is simple and straightforward, without any side-issues from the main track. After Act I our whole attention is focused on the love of Romeo and Juliet.

The way Shakespeare speeds up the action gives dramatic concentration. It emphasizes the suddenness of the love of Romeo and Juliet, love at first sight, aroused in a moment and soon to be opposed. But notwithstanding this, Act I leans forward and would do with clipping back; the talk about Rosaline could with advantage be cut down. All that is necessary is that the audience should realize the power of their mutual love to reverse the previous trend of their life, when Romeo was in love with someone else and Juliet unaffected by love. The play proper does not begin until Act I, Scene v, and Scenes ii, iii and iv (at this length) reduce the dramatic concentration and are slow by comparison with the rest.

an introduction
to the tragedy
of Romeo & Juliet

The climax, the marriage of hero and heroine, comes early in the play. Act III, Scene i is the turning point, and thereafter the fortunes of Romeo and Juliet quickly go downhill until the catastrophe in the last scene. Mercutio's witty tongue was getting him more attention than Romeo's so he is removed, and at the same time his death provides a reason for Romeo to take Tybalt's life and so run himself into banishment. The two duels are Shakespeare's means of bringing these events about.

In any play there is a clash of personalities or of wills. It is this that makes the play. Notice the clash in this play between age and youth, between Capulets and Montagues in general, which itself contrasts with the passionate love of two of the young members of these houses, between the Prince and these rebellious families, and, in particular, between Romeo's affected love for Rosaline and his real love for Juliet, between the love of Paris and of Romeo for Juliet, between Mercutio and Tybalt, Romeo and Tybalt, Juliet and her parents (and later her nurse), and between Romeo and his friends owing to his absorption in love, especially between Mercutio's wit and Romeo's. Contrast is a fundamental principle in Shakespearean drama, and the student should notice how the play is constructed to bring about such contrasts.

There is very little comic relief in *Romeo and Juliet.* The garrulous chatter of the Nurse and the talk of the musicians after they have found that they are not wanted are the only examples in the play of more than a line or two. Mercutio's witty repartee is on a higher plane than the Nurse's common gossip.

Much in the play depends on coincidence, but particularly in the last two scenes: the Friar's letter never reached Romeo, Paris happened to come to the tomb at the same time as Romeo, and Romeo kills himself only a few minutes before Juliet awakes. The greater element of chance in *Romeo and Juliet* makes the events seem less related to the character of the principals than in Shakespeare's later plays. Their fate is not so much caused by their own actions and characters.

As usual in Shakespeare's plays there is little attention to detail. The effect of the Friar's potion was to wear off after "two and forty hours" (a most exact time — not "about two days"), yet Juliet is asleep after fifty hours and the Friar, who expected her to awake after forty-two hours and might well have made sure by being there before, fails to arrive until some eight or nine hours later than this.

But students should remember that details like this, which are noticed when one reads the play, comparing passage with passage, would go unnoticed by an audience in the theater. Shakespeare constructed his plays without re-

gard for gritty little details, but with much regard for their general pattern.

It is but seldom that Shakespeare uses a Prologue (or Chorus). Shakespeare's usual method is to set the scene for the audience in the conversation of minor characters before the principals enter, which makes the play seem more real. He follows this method here, too, and the Prologues to Acts I and II are not really necessary.

ATMOSPHERE AND THEME

The theme of *Romeo and Juliet* is a consuming love. It is a story of hatred overcome by that love, old hate versus young love, taking no thought for the past or the future, and this love ends in "love-devouring."

The atmosphere is one of passion and swiftness, full-blooded passion and rash swiftness. Consuming love calls for haste— "Gallop apace, you fiery-footed steeds." "From nine till twelve is three long hours." The whole play is in a hurry—speed into marriage, speed into banishment, speed back to Juliet, speed in another quarter to get Juliet married to Paris, speed to kill whoever steps in the way and speed to commit suicide when life suddenly seems not worth living. Romeo's haste makes him happy in his marriage, and immediately thereafter unhappy in his banishment. *Romeo and Juliet* is a play of whirlwind and storm, full of angry feud, tremendous passion and sudden death.

Even when things are going well there is a sense of impending tragedy in the air, a grim foreboding that makes happy folk mistrust their happiness. The first Prologue speaks of "A pair of star-cross'd lovers" before the play proper starts. The first scene of the play shows how affairs are like powder waiting for a match, and there are those only too glad to bring one. There is a nameless dread before Romeo has ever set eyes on Juliet, and after they have met, both have a presentiment that their love shall end in disaster. Romeo comes to marry Juliet with a challenge to fate on his lips — "Then love-devouring death do what he dare." And Juliet, as she looks on Romeo (alive) for the last time, admits:

O God, I have an ill-diving soul!
Methinks I see them, now thou art below.
As one dead in the bottom of a tomb.

These hints of tragedy increase the suspense (and the irony) of the play.

Most of Shakespeare's tragedies end on a note of hope, and this, the first, strikes the pattern of the rest. The lives of these lovers are burnt up, but the final effect of the play is not wholly pessimistic. It would have been had their deaths increased the hatred of the Montagues and Capulets. But at the end the heads of these two houses shake hands over the "poor sacrifices of their enmity." The tragedy has left things better than they were at the start of the play.

The great majority of Shakespeare's scenes (apart from those in the Histories) are set in places abroad, a device which of itself gave them a romantic coloring. But the local color of all his plays is that of Elizabethan England, whether the story is one of Italy, Egypt, or Denmark. Nowadays we should demand strict accuracy in scenery, costumes and topical references, but then, for playwright and audience alike, the life and spirit of a play mattered more than strict accuracy in local color. "It is the spirit which giveth life." People saw in the drama a reflection of their own life and experience; its appeal was in no way analytical or educational, but human.

Further, in those days people were untraveled and uneducated, and anachronisms would not strike a false note in an age more familiar with stories than with their setting. Only a very few privileged persons could know (by travel or study) what Italian cities were really like, so that the incongruity of the local color would pass unnoticed.

Romeo and Juliet takes place nominally in Verona (one scene in Mantua). Although pomegranate trees and ducats are mentioned, we are really never very far from the England Shakespeare knew. The local color is essentially Elizabethan.

13

Capulet is represented as "the great rich Capulet," but his household is that of a regular Elizabethan lord of the manor—small enough, indeed, for Lord and Lady to be at hand immediately when the Nurse calls them from their daughter's bedroom. The kitchen staff is unable to cope with the great occasion, and the Nurse helps in the pantry and the Lord stays up all night and sees that there are enough dry logs for the fire.

On the wedding morning the bridegroom is to go early to awake the bride with music and take her to church for the ceremony, the Elizabethan way of doing things.

There were no tombs such as that in Act V, Scene iii, in Shakespeare's England. This massive vault is not due to a sudden desire for Italian local color, however, it is simply that the scene could not be represented otherwise.

Some people say that the hot days and moonlit nights, and, above all, the impetuous passion, give the play an Italian setting. But are there no hot days and moonlit nights in England? As for full-blooded passion, in Shakespeare's plays this is by no means reserved for men and women of Italian, or any other, race.

an introduction to the tragedy of Romeo & Juliet

STYLE

Romeo and Juliet is very different from Shakespeare's later plays in containing so much rhyme, much of it alternate rhyme. The introduction of the passages in sonnet form (e.g. the first words between Romeo and Juliet) is also an indication of an early play. The sonnet was, however, a recognized medium for the language of love in Elizabethan England and is, therefore, not unfitting in that particular place.

The normal line in Shakespeare's plays is a blank verse iambic pentameter. There is much variation, however, making the verse more interesting to listen to and the dialogue more adapted to different characters. But there is not so much variation in the line of *Romeo and Juliet* as in those of later plays, and most of the lines are end-stopped, another sign of an early play.

Graphic and figurative language abounds, and the richness, vividness and variety of the imagery is to be noted. Nowhere in Shakespeare is there more lovely poetry than in *Romeo and Juliet*, nowhere is there more warmth and beauty and tenderness than in Act II. The similes and metaphors have that sense of surprise and yet of fitness which characterizes the imagery of a genius.

Not only is there beauty in the imagery of the poetry, but the sound of many passages comes "like softest music to attending ears" (notice the beautiful alliteration in this very passage, giving the "silver-sweet" sound of which it is speaking). Alliteration is often used with onomatopoeic effect, for example the deadness of the d's in "Then love-devouring death do what he dare."

In Elizabethan times punning was extremely popular, and punning is second nature to nearly every character in the play. Much of the point of this witty repartee is lost on a modern audience. Indeed, it is not necessary for the modern audience to understand the exact point of Mercutio's jokes, so long as the general fun and frolic and nonsense comes over.

In a good play the style naturally reflects the character of the person speaking, and even the same man in two different moods may speak in two different ways. Contrast the airy tone of Mercutio's famous "Queen Mab" speech (I.iv), light as a soap bubble, with the staid speeches of the Prince and Friar Laurence — or even Benvolio. Look at Capulet's long speech in Act I, Scene ii, and contrast this with his jerky, disjointed speech when his temper is up (III.v), or when he is fussily hurrying about giving orders for the wedding feast (IV.iv).

Nearly one-eighth of *Romeo and Juliet* is in prose. When prose is used in Shakespeare's plays it is for a definite purpose. Prose is invariably the language

of comic characters and characters of lower social position. This was a literary convention at a time when literature was aristocratic and the chief characters in plays (as in life) were kings and nobles. Scenes in which the lower orders of society figure are a contrast; these people live on a lower plane of feeling than the main characters, and thereby emphasize the height of the feeling of the main characters, and the contrast in the medium of expression, prose instead of verse—is in perfect keeping.

In Act I, Scene i the servants talk in prose and those of noble family in verse, and this distinction is kept throughout the play. Sometimes the reason for prose is a lower pitch of feeling without a lower social position in the speaker, for example the jocular talk of Benvolio, Mercutio and Romeo in Act II, Scene iv. But when Benvolio and Mercutio have gone, Romeo thinks of Juliet and tells the Nurse in verse of the plans he has made to marry her. In the following scene the Nurse (who probably speaks in verse anywhere only owing to her close association with Juliet) alternates between verse and prose according to the tone of her speech—whether it is concerned with the matter in hand or is just bantering prattle from nurse to child. Similarly in III.i the emotional pitch determines whether prose or verse shall be the medium. In the last act of the Apothecary and the

Watch no doubt speak in verse because they are caught up in great events. Juliet always speaks in verse.

Formal communications (e.g. the list of people invited to Capulet's mask) are, of course, in prose.

DRAMATIC IRONY

In *Romeo and Juliet* Shakespeare makes full use of dramatic irony—the difference between the situation as known to the audience and as supposed by the characters of the play or by some of them. The basis of dramatic irony is ambiguity of meaning. A remark may have a surface meaning for the characters in the play but an added signification for the audience. The double meaning may be intended by the speaker or just casual. The secrecy of the marriage of Romeo and Juliet lends itself to dramatic irony. When Lady Capulet is denouncing Romeo, Juliet appears to agree with her, but her phrases are double-edged:

Ay, madam, from the reach of these my hands:
Would none but I might venge my cousin's death!

Indeed, I never shall be satisfied
With Romeo, till I behold him
—dead—
Is my poor heart so for a kinsman vex'd.

When Romeo has fallen in love with Juliet, Mercutio imagines that he is still moping for Rosaline.

Ah, that same pale hardhearted wench, that Rosaline,
Torments him so that he will sure run mad.

Similarly, Lady Capulet imagines that Juliet is upset owing to Tybalt's murder (III.iv.11). The Nurse tells Juliet of a "bloody piteous corse," and Juliet, thinking that it must be Romeo's exclaims, "And thou and Romeo press one heavy bier!" Little did she think when she spoke these words that they would be made true. In answer to Juliet's last words to him, "O, think'st thou we shall ever meet again?" Romeo says, "I doubt it not." So it was, but not in the sense in which he meant it.

Lady Capulet plans her revenge on Romeo by "an unaccustom'd dram, that he shall soon keep Tybalt company," and so does it fall out, but not by her ordering.

Dramatis Personae

ESCALUS, Prince of Verona.

PARIS, a young Nobleman, Kinsman to the Prince.

MONTAGUE
CAPULET } Heads of two Houses at variance with each other.

Uncle to Capulet.

ROMEO, son to Montague.

MERCUTIO, kinsman to the Prince
BENVOLIO, nephew to Montague } Friends to Romeo.

TYBALT, nephew to Lady Capulet.

FRIAR LAURENCE, a Franciscan.

FRIAR JOHN, of the same Order.

BALTHASAR, servant to Romeo

SAMPSON
GREGORY } servants to Capulet.

PETER, servant to Juliet's nurse.

ABRAHAM, servant to Montague.

An Apothecary.

Three Musicians.

Page to Mercutio.

Page to Paris.

Another Page.

An Officer.

LADY MONTAGUE, wife to Montague.

LADY CAPULET, wife to Capulet.

JULIET, daughter to Capulet.

Nurse to Juliet.

Citizens of Verona; male and female Kinsfolk to both Houses;
Maskers, Guards, Watchmen and Attendants.

Chorus.

SCENE—*Verona: Once (in the Fifth Act), at Mantua.*

ROMEO AND JULIET

PROLOGUE TO ACT I

This opening speech serves as an introduction, or program, to the play, but seems unnecessary to most modern audiences. It is usually delivered by a single narrator (usually one of the other characters in the play) but was intended to be spoken by a chorus of voices. In form, this prologue resembles a Shakespearean sonnet with fourteen lines and a rhyming couplet at the end. The Prologue is not included in the Folio version, and may have been inserted by a later writer despite the oft-quoted lines relating to the "pair of star-cross'd lovers" and the "two hours' traffic of our stage." The Prologue directs our attention to the important part fate plays in the lives of the two young lovers, who are at least to some extent the victims of their parents' strife. Thus their love is described as being "death-mark'd." The "loins of these two foes," i.e., of the two families concerned, are "fatal" for the offspring of them. Fate lowers over all, as in a Greek tragedy. The end is prefigured in the beginning with tragic inevitability. The use of a Chorus reinforces the resemblance to a Greek tragedy, and came down to Shakespeare through the Latin plays of Seneca and the English imitations of classical drama, like the tragedy of GORBODUC (c. 1560). Shakespeare employed choruses in only one of the tragedies, but in three other plays, namely HENRY V, HENRY VIII, and TROILUS AND CRESSIDA.

The point of this Prologue is to make it clear that the fate of the two young lovers is not their fault, but their misfortune, for which they were not entirely responsible.

ACT I SCENE I

The setting is the Market Place in the Italian city of Verona on a Sunday morning, about one hour before daybreak in July. On the stage are two of the minor characters, Sampson and Gregory, and they open the play with some crude and lively repartee delivered at a rapid rate. It was not unusual for Shakespeare to open a play with minor characters. Sampson and Gregory are armed servants belonging to the house of Capulet. They have inherited, or acquired, their master's feud against the other leading house, the Montagues. They boast of their quickness and dexterity in rapier fighting and describe the enemy house and its members and servants in very unfavorable terms. They are high-spirited and full of life, and not unintelligent. For ex-

---

THE PROLOGUE

Enter Chorus.

Chorus. Two households, both alike in dignity,   1
    In fair Verona, where we lay our scene,
From ancient grudge break to new mutiny,   3
    Where civil blood makes civil hands unclean.   4
From forth the fatal loins of these two foes   5
    A pair of star-crossed lovers take their life;   6
Whose misadventured piteous overthrows   7
Doth with their death bury their parents' strife.
The fearful passage of their death-marked love,   9
    And the continuance of their parents' rage,
Which, but their children's end, naught could
    remove,
Is now the two hours' traffic of our stage;   12
The which of you with patient ears attend,
What here shall miss, our toil shall strive to mend.   14
        [*Exeunt.*

ACT ONE, scene one.

(VERONA. A PUBLIC PLACE)

Enter SAMPSON *and* GREGORY, *with swords and bucklers, of the house of Capulet.*

Sampson. Gregory, on my word, we'll not carry coals.   1
Gregory. No, for then we should be colliers.   2
Sampson. I mean, an we be in choler, we'll draw.   3
Gregory. Ay, while you live, draw your neck out of collar.
Sampson. I strike quickly, being moved.
Gregory. But thou are not quickly moved to strike.   6
Sampson. A dog of the house of Montague moves me.   7
Gregory. To move is to stir, and to be valiant is to stand. Therefore, if thou art moved, thou runn'st away.
Sampson. A dog of that house shall move me to stand. I will take the wall of any man or maid of   11
Montague's.
Gregory. That shows thee a weak slave; for the weakest goes to the wall.   13
Sampson. 'Tis true; and therefore women, being the weaker vessels, are ever thrust to the wall. There-   15
fore I will push Montague's men from the wall and thrust his maids to the wall.
Gregory. The quarrel is between our masters, and us their men.
Sampson. 'Tis all one. I will show myself a tyrant.   20
When I have fought with the men, I will be cruel with the maids—I will cut off their heads.
Gregory. The heads of the maids?
Sampson. Ay, the heads of the maids, or their maidenheads. Take it in what sense thou wilt.
Gregory. They must take it in sense that feel it.

---

1. "alike": equal.
   "households": the Capulets and the Montagues.

3. "mutiny": disorder, tumult—between anyone, not just in the armed forces.

4. "civil blood makes civil hands unclean": the blood of the citizens in civil war makes the hands of a civilized (well-mannered) people unclean. (Metonymy and synecdoche)

5. "fatal": i.e., destined to produce issue fated for misfortune.

6. "star-crossed": i.e., their fortunes were marred by the influence of the stars. That men's natures and fortunes were influenced by the star under which they were born was a widespread superstition of Elizabethan times.

7-8. "Whose . . . strife": the cessation of whose unfortunate pitiful struggles makes an end to their parents' strife. "Overthrows" is a noun, not a verb.

9. "death-marked": destined (marked out) for death.

12. "traffic": business, concern.

14. "miss": fail, be missing, perhaps an implied metaphor, i.e., miss the mark.

1. "carry coals": submit to insult, like servants.

2. "colliers": workmen who carry and trade in coal.

3. "an we be in choler": if we are angry, if our blood is up.
   "draw": draw swords (note pun on carrying a collar equipped with buckets for drawing water from a well).

6. "moved": roused to anger, stirred.

7. "A dog": i.e., any low-down fellow.

11. "take the wall of": prove superiority by fighting with back to the wall.

13. "goes to the wall": i.e., the other extreme, is pushed against the wall.

15. "thrust to the wall": a sexual joke.

20. " 'Tis all one": i.e., 'tis all the same, it makes no difference to me.

ROMEO AND JULIET

ACT I SCENE I

ample, Gregory has the wit to perceive that "the quarrel is between our masters and us their men." Gregory would probably have been an advocate of strike action if he had lived in the age of the trade unions. There is some discussion as to strength and weakness, and some characteristic sexual humor which the Elizabethans took in their stride. Sampson boasts of his tyranny and of his cruelty, but we take all this with a pinch of salt.

Abraham and Balthasar, two armed servants of the rival house of Montague, enter at this point. Sampson's "naked weapon," (his rapier) is drawn, and he is ready for a quarrel. He advises his fellow-servant Gregory, to let the Montagues attack first, so that the law will be on the Capulet side if they are forced to defend themselves.

An amusing though potentially violent altercation ensues, during which Sampson and Gregory try to keep on the right side of the law while being as offensive to the Montague servants as possible. Since they are not certain what the law permits, their anxiety is all the greater and therefore the more amusing. Gregory warns Sampson that one of his master's relatives is approaching, and Benvolio, whose name means "Good-natured man," enters.

Benvolio beats down their swords, and tells them to "part, fools!" Tybalt enters. He is Lady Capulet's nephew, and the Capulet servants respect him. Montague's nephew, Benvolio, has his sword drawn, and says he was trying to break up the fight among the servants, which is true; but the fiery Tybalt does not believe that a man whose weapon is drawn can be trying to keep the peace, so he threatens him to fight for his life. Tybalt says he hates all Montagues, including Benvolio, and they fight.

Several other persons from both the rival houses enter, and join in the fray, until there is a scene of widespread disorder. The Citizens then enter, carrying clubs and long-handled spears equipped with blades, and crying "Down with the Capulets! Down with the Montagues!" At this moment, the father of the house of Capulet enters accompanied by Lady Capulet. The old lord cries out for his sword, but his wife says a crutch would suit him better. He is quite ancient, and rather frail now, but full of hatred for his rivals, particularly the ancient leader of the house of Montague, his opposite number.

Sampson. Me they shall feel while I am able to stand; and 'tis known I am a pretty piece of flesh.

Gregory. 'Tis well thou art not fish; if thou hadst, thou hadst been poor-John. Draw thy tool! Here comes two of the house of Montagues.

Enter two other Servingmen. ABRAM AND BALTHASAR.

Sampson. My naked weapon is out. Quarrel! I will back thee.

Gregory. How? turn thy back and run?

Sampson. Fear me not.

Gregory. No, marry. I fear thee!   36

Sampson. Let us take the law of our sides; let them 37
begin.

Gregory. I will frown as I pass by, and let them take it as they list.   39

Sampson. Nay, as they dare. I will bite my thumb 40
at them, which is disgrace to them if they bear it.

Abram. Do you bite your thumb at us, sir?

Sampson. I do bite my thumb, sir.

Abram. Do you bite your thumb at us, sir?

Sampson. [*aside to* GREGORY] Is the law of our side if I say ay?

Gregory. [*aside to* SAMPSON] No.

Sampson. No, sir, I do not bite my thumb at you, sir; but I bite my thumb, sir.

Gregory. Do you quarrel, sir?

Abram. Quarrel, sir? No, sir.

Sampson. But if you do, sir, I am for you. I serve 51
as good a man as you.

Abram. No better.

Sampson. Well, sir.   54

Enter BENVOLIO.

Gregory [*aside to* SAMPSON] Say 'better.' Here comes one of my master's kinsmen.   56

Sampson. Yes, better, sir.

Abram. You lie.

Sampson. Draw, if you be men. Gregory, remember thy swashing blow.   [*They fight.* 60

Benvolio. Part, fools!
Put up your swords. You know not what you do.

Enter TYBALT.

Tybalt. What, art thou drawn among these heart- 63
less hinds?
Turn thee, Benvolio! look upon thy death.

Benvolio. I do but keep the peace. Put up thy sword,
Or manage it to part these men with me.   66

Tybalt. What, drawn, and talk of peace? I hate the word
As I hate hell, all Montagues, and thee.
Have at thee, coward!   [*They fight.* 69

Enter an Officer, *and three or four* Citizens *with clubs or partisans.*

Officer. Clubs, bills, and partisans! Strike! beat 70
them down!

Citizens. Down with the Capulets! Down with the Montagues!

Enter old CAPULET *in his gown, and his* Wife.

Capulet. What noise is this? Give me my long 73
sword, ho!

36. "marry": an oath-LIT "by the Virgin Mary," but in effect no stronger than "indeed."

37. "take the law of our sides": make sure we have the law on our side.

39. "list": choose, please.

40. "bite my thumb": an insulting gesture in Shakespeare's time.

Friser le pouce

51. "I am for you": I accept your challenge, ready to fight you.

54. "Well, sir": Sampson cannot understand what Abraham means by his non-committal reply. He could mean that there was no better master than his own or that there was no better master than Sampson's.

56. "one of my master's kinsmen": Tybalt; evidently he does not see Benvolio.

60. "swashing blow": knock-out blow, let a blow that comes down with a swishing noise.

63. "heartless hinds": cowardly servants (pun on hinds [deer] without a male leader, or hart).

66. "manage": employ, use.

69. "Have at thee": on guard!

70. "Clubs": the cry of the London apprentices to call their fellows, sometimes to come with their clubs to keep the peace, as often as not to create a disturbance.
"bills": long wooden staves with a blade or axe-head at one end.
"partisans": long infantry spears.

73. "long sword": i.e., sword for action, not one to be worn merely for fashion's sake.

ROMEO AND JULIET

ACT I SCENE I

The disturbance becomes a full-scale riot aided and abetted by the nobles present, who should have used their seniority and rank to try to restore the peace. Their dereliction of duty shows us that hostile emotions rather than reason govern them, and when they confront one another the Capulets and the Montagues become infuriated with one aim, to kill the enemy.

Capulet spies old Montague approaching, flourishing his sword blade at him, and he determines to give battle. Lady Montague tries to hold her lord back, but he shakes her off and tries to advance but she again prevents him.

Suddenly the Prince of Verona, Escalus, enters and intervenes. He calls them all "rebellious subjects, enemies to peace," and after admonishing them severely, warns them that if they ever disturb the civil peace of Verona again, they will pay for it with their lives. Escalus dismisses the crowd and tells everybody to go home; he takes Capulet along. He will see Montague in the afternoon. He will discuss with each the measures he will take if the peace is broken again.

All exit, except old Montague, his wife, and Benvolio. Montague asks Benvolio what started the fight this time, and Benvolio replies that the servants of the two rival families were "close fighting" before Benvolio got there; Benvolio drew his sword to part them when the "fiery Tybalt" entered and started fighting Benvolio until they were in turn parted by the arrival of the Prince and his train.

Lady Montague expresses considerable relief that her son, Romeo, was not present at this fray. This is the first reference to Romeo in the play, and he has not yet appeared on the stage. We gather that he is impetuous and would not have hesitated to join in the fighting had he been there.

Where was Romeo while the disturbance in the Market Place of Verona was taking place? He was walking early in the woods, and evidently wanted to be alone. Benvolio saw him there, but did not intrude on Romeo's privacy.

Montague says that Romeo has been showing signs of disturbance, probably emotional. He has been weeping, and stealing home to pen himself up in his room alone, with the windows shut to make an artificial night.

Benvolio asks his uncle if he knows why Romeo behaves like

Wife. A crutch, a crutch! Why call you for a sword?
Capulet. My sword, I say! Old Montague is come
And flourishes his blade in spite of me. 76

Enter old MONTAGUE *and his* Wife.

Montague. Thou villain Capulet!—Hold me not, let me go.
Montague's Wife. Thou shalt not stir one foot to seek a foe.

Enter PRINCE ESCALUS, *with his Train.*

Prince. Rebellious subjects, enemies to peace,
Profaners of this neighbor-stained steel— 80
Will they not hear? What, ho! you men, you beasts,
That quench the fire of your pernicious rage
With purple fountains issuing from your veins!
On pain of torture, from those bloody hands
Throw your mistempered weapons to the ground 85
And hear the sentence of your moved prince. 86
Three civil brawls, bred of an airy word 87
By thee, old Capulet, and Montague,
Have thrice disturbed the quiet of our streets
And made Verona's ancient citizens
Cast by their grave beseeming ornaments 91
To wield old partisans, in hands as old, 92
Cank'red with peace, to part your cank'red hate. 93
If ever you disturb our streets again,
Your lives shall pay the forfeit of the peace.
For this time all the rest depart away.
You, Capulet, shall go along with me;
And, Montague, come you this afternoon,
To know our farther pleasure in this case, 99
To old Freetown, our common judgment place. 100
Once more, on pain of death, all men depart.
[*Exeunt all but* MONTAGUE, *his* wife, *and* BENVOLIO.
Montague Who set this ancient quarrel new abroach? 102
Speak, nephew, were you by when it began?
Benvolio. Here were the servants of your adversary
And yours, close fighting ere I did approach. 105
I drew to part them. In the instant came
The fiery Tybalt, with his sword prepared;
Which, as he breathed defiance to my ears,
He swung about his head and cut the winds,
Who, nothing hurt withal, hissed him in scorn. 110
While we were interchanging thrusts and blows,
Came more and more, and fought on part and part, 112
Till the Prince came, who parted either part. 113
Montague's Wife. O, where is Romeo? Saw you him to-day?
Right glad I am he was not at this fray.
Benvolio. Madam, an hour before the worshipped sun
Peered forth the golden window of the East,
A troubled mind drave me to walk abroad;
Where, underneath the grove of sycamore 119
That westward rooteth from this city side, 120
So early walking did I see your son.
Towards him I made, but he was ware of me
And stole into the covert of the wood.
I, measuring his affections by my own,

76. "in spite of me": to defy me.

80. "Profaners . . . steel": i.e., you profane your weapons by staining them with the blood of your neighbors.

85. "mistempered": tempered for an evil end.

86. "moved": angry.

87. "bred . . . word": arising out of words lightly spoken.

91. "beseeming ornaments": weapons befitting them (i.e., walkingsticks).

92. "To": in order to.

93. "Cank'red . . . cankered": rusty, malignant (a canker is a bud-destroying worm; hence cancer).

99. "our farther pleasure": what also we wish to do. The "our" is the royal plural, used throughout the speech.

100. "Freetown": the 'Villa Franca' of an old poem by Brooke, which in the poem was the name of Capulet's castle.

102. "new abroach": newly afoot (newly under way).

105. "close": i.e., in the thick of a fight.

110. "Who": antecedent "the winds." "nothing hurt withal": not at all hurt thereby.
"hissed him in scorn": refers to the swish of his sword through the air.

112. "on part": on one side or the other.

113. "parted either part": separated both sides.

119. "sycamore": traditionally associated with disappointed lovers.

120. "westward . . . side": grows on the west side of the city.

ROMEO AND JULIET

ACT I SCENE I

this, and Montague says Romeo will not tell him. Romeo refuses to disclose the reasons for his disturbance to any of the friends who have attempted to find out. If they knew the cause, they would know how to solve the problem.

Romeo is seen approaching, and Montague and his wife leave in the hope that Benvolio will be able to know what Romeo's grievance is. On entering we see Romeo is young and melancholy, but handsome and beneath his temporary lassitude of vigorous disposition. He asks if that was his father who went out so quickly. He does not miss much, evidently. Romeo confesses that he is out of favor with the girl with whom he is in love. This is what distresses him. He sees signs of the fray that recently took place in the Market Place, and asks what caused it, but quickly prevents an answer by saying he knows what happened: "Here's much to do with hate, but more with love." He knows the family feud was responsible for the outbreak, but suggests something deeper even than this is involved. His following list of contradictory and opposed elements, including the oxymoron "loving hate," indicates his deep personal upset.

Romeo realizes that he is probably a humorous object to others, but Benvolio is very understanding and sympathetic, as a friend should be, and commiserates with him. Romeo leaves, after talking rather wildly of the grief of love and its sorrows and delights. He makes it clear that he is experiencing only the sorrows at present. Benvolio offers to go along, and asks Romeo who he loves. Romeo fences with his question, and says he loves, in sadness, a woman. This does not deter Benvolio, who is very patient.

Romeo and Benvolio play with words while they discuss Romeo's problem, which is that the girl with whom he is in love will not allow him or anybody else to woo her. In this she deprives all, including posterity (since she cannot have any heirs unless she consents to yield up her chastity first). Although all this banter is light-hearted, Romeo clearly is suffering all the pangs of passionate unrequited love.

Benvolio advises Romeo to forget her. Romeo says you might as well teach me to forget to think. He is obsessed by her beauty, and cannot forget her charms. He makes another passionate speech, then leaves Benvolio, presumably to go and mope in his room thinking of the favors he is so cruelly denied.

Which then most sought where most might not be found,
Being one too many by my weary self,
Pursued my humor, not pursuing his, 127
And gladly shunned who gladly fled from me. 128
   Montague. Many a morning hath he there been seen,
With tears augmenting the fresh morning's dew,
Adding to clouds more clouds with his deep sighs;
But all so soon as the all-cheering sun
Should in the farthest East begin to draw
The shady curtains from Aurora's bed, 134
Away from light steals home my heavy son 135
And private in his chamber pens himself,
Shuts up his windows, locks fair daylight out,
And makes himself an artificial night.
Black and portentous must this humor prove 139
Unless good counsel may the cause remove.
   Benvolio. My noble uncle, do you know the cause?
   Montague. I neither know it nor can learn of him.
   Benvolio. Have you importuned him by any means? 143
   Montague. Both by myself and many other friends;
But he, his own affections' counsellor, 145
Is to himself—I will not say how true— 146
But to himself so secret and so close,
So far from sounding and discovery, 148
As is the bud bit with an envious worm 149
Ere he can spread his sweet leaves to the air
Or dedicate his beauty to the sun.
Could we but learn from whence his sorrows grow,
We would as willingly give cure as know. 153
            Enter ROMEO.
   Benvolio. See, where he comes. So please you step aside,
I'll know his grievance, or be much denied. 155
   Montague. I would thou wert so happy by thy stay
To hear true shrift. Come, madam, let's away. 157
           [*Exeunt* MONTAGUE *and* Wife.
   Benvolio. Good morrow, cousin.
   Romeo.   Is the day so young?
   Benvolio. But new struck nine.
   Romeo.   Ay me! sad hours seem long.
Was that my father that went hence so fast?
   Benvolio. It was. What sadness lengthens Romeo's hours?
   Romeo. Not having that which having makes them short.
   Benvolio. In love?
   Romeo. Out—
   Benvolio. Of love?
   Romeo. Out of her favor where I am in love. 166
   Benvolio. Alas that love, so gentle in his view, 167
Should be so tyrannous and rough in proof! 168
   Romeo. Alas that love, whose view is muffled still,
Should without eyes see pathways to his will! 170
Where shall we dine? O me! What fray was here?
Yet tell me not, for I have heard it all.
Here's much to do with hate, but more with love. 173
Why then, O brawling love, O loving hate, 174
O anything, of nothing first create!
O heavy lightness, serious vanity,

127. "humor": inclination of the title of Ben Johnson's play "Every Man in His Humour" (i.e., according to his mood, temperament or disposition).

128. "shunned": takes the object (understand) him.

134. "Aurora's": goddess of dawn—in classical mythology.

135. "heavy": sad (note pun on "light").

139. "portentous": boding evil—ominous, threatening.

143. "importuned": persistent, asking.

145. "his own . . . counsellor": admitting to himself alone.

146. "true": i.e., true to himself.

148. "sounding": being fathomed.

149. "bud . . . worm": never opening to be overseen.
"envious": malignant.

153. "know": i.e., know what the trouble is.
"enter Romeo": dramatically it is much more effective to "lead up" to Romeo like this, in the conversation of minor characters, than to bring him on the stage at the outset. This method has the advantage of creating suspense, and when the main character appears, he appears in response to a longing of the audience to see him. Our imagination has been worked upon by the talk of Benvolio, Montague and his Lady, so that when Romeo appears he already has our interest. From a practical point of view it also means that the first speeches of the main character are not disturbed by the entry of latercomers: by the time he speaks, the audience has settled down.

155. "be much denied": force him to give me a strong refusal.

157. "shrift": confession.

166. "where": with whom.

167. "in his view": in appearance ('his' effects the personification).

168. "in proof": in experience—reality.

170. "his will": i.e., make people fall in love. Cupid, the god of love, was represented as blind in classical mythology.

173. "to do": trouble.
"more with love": perhaps because Rosaline belonged to the Capulet family (as we see from the list of invited guests, Sc. II), or he may mean that there is more in his heart to do with love.

174. "loving hate": this and the following pairings of opposites are examples of the figure of speech known as oxymoron.

ROMEO AND JULIET

ACT I SCENE I

The shallowness of Romeo's love for Rosaline is revealed by the artificiality of the language describing her beauty and his love. By describing love in a dozen contradictory terms he reveals the intellectual rather than emotional basis of his affection.

The reference to Diana, the chaste goddess of hunting and of the moon, is probably a poetic compliment to Queen Elizabeth I, who took pride in her virgin state. This is supported by the fact that Shakespeare deplores the fact that in spite of offers of marriage, she had decided to remain single, so that her excellence would not be passed on to future sovereigns.

An oracular note is contained in the veiled prophecy of what is to take place in Benvolio's affirmation that he will teach Romeo to forget his love, or die in the attempt. Shortly afterwards this prophecy is fulfilled (when Mercutio is killed in the duel provoked by Romeo's discovery of his new love, Juliet).

The dramatic purposes of this scene are fivefold:

1. The street-fighting captures the attention of the audience, and reveals the extent and seriousness of the family feud.

2. All the leading characters of the play, except Mercutio and Juliet, are introduced to the audience for the first time.

3. The time and scene (setting) of the play are announced, and the action, dress, talk and dispositions of the characters are established.

4. The basic conflict which is the theme of this tragedy is revealed in the romance that is threatened by a family feud.

5. Benvolio's prophecy of his own death, and the taking place of this death so soon afterwards, prepares the audience for further tragic developments in connection with some other characters in this play.

Misshapen chaos of well-seeming forms,
Feather of lead, bright smoke, cold fire, sick health,
Still-waking sleep, that is not what it is! 179
This love feel I, that feel no love in this. 180
Dost thou not laugh?
Benvolio. No, coz, I rather weep. 181
Romeo. Good heart, at what?
Benvolio. At thy good heart's oppression.
Romeo. Why, such is love's transgression 183
Griefs of mine own lie heavy in my breast,
Which thou wilt propagate, to have it prest 185
With more of thine. This love that thou hast shown 186
Doth add more grief to too much of mine own.
Love is a smoke raised with the fume of sighs;
Being purged, a fire sparkling in lovers' eyes;
Being vexed, a sea nourished with lovers' tears.
What is it else? A madness most discreet,
A choking gall, and a preserving sweet. 192
Farewell, my coz.
Benvolio. Soft! I will go along. 193
An if you leave me so, you do me wrong.
Romeo. Tut! I have lost myself; I am not here;
This is not Romeo, he's some other where.
Benvolio. Tell me in sadness, who is that you love? 197
Romeo. What, shall I groan and tell thee? 198
Benvolio. Groan? Why, no;
But sadly tell me who.
Romeo. Bid a sick man in sadness make his will.
Ah, word ill urged to one that is so ill! 201
In sadness, cousin, I do love a woman.
Benvolio. I aimed so near when I supposed you 203
loved.
Romeo. A right good markman. And she's fair I love.
Benvolio. A right fair mark, fair coz, is soonest hit. 205
Romeo. Well, in that hit you miss. She'll not be hit
With Cupid's arrow. She hath Dian's wit, 207
And, in strong proof of chastity well armed,
From Love's weak childish bow she lives unharmed.
She will not stay the siege of loving terms, 210
Nor bide th' encounter of assailing eyes, 211
Nor ope her lap to saint-seducing gold.
O, she is rich in beauty; only poor
That, when she dies, with beauty dies her store. 214
Benvolio. Then she hath sworn that she will live
chaste?
Romeo. She hath, and in that sparing makes huge
waste;
For beauty, starved with her severity,
Cuts beauty off from all posterity.
She is too fair, too wise, wisely too fair,
To merit bliss by making me despair. 220
She hath forsworn to love, and in that vow 221
Do I live dead that live to tell it now. 222
Benvolio. Be he ruled by me; forget to think of her. 223
Romeo. O, teach me how I should forget to think! 224
Benvolio. By giving liberty unto thine eyes.
Examine other beauties.
Romeo. 'Tis the way
To call hers (exquisite) in question more.
These happy masks that kiss fair ladies' brows,

179. "Still-waking": keeping awake all the time.

180. "no love": i.e., no really satisfying love.

181. "coz": cousin (any relative or close friend).

183. "transgression": in making lovers suffer so.

185. "propagate": increase.
"to have it prest": by having it oppressed.

186. "thine": i.e., thy griefs.

192. "A choking . . . sweet": a substance bitter enough to choke (anyone) and sweet enough to preserve (something).

193. "Soft": a common exclamation of Shakespeare's time, equivalent to "Wait a minute!"

197. "in sadness": seriously.

198. "groan": Romeo purposely misunderstands "sadness," as if used in its modern sense—"Shall I groan in sadness?"

201. "ill urged": a suggestion made at an inopportune time.

203. "aimed so near": guessed, as much (Benvolio wants to know which woman Romeo loves).

205. "fair mark" clear target. Benvolio plays on the word "fair" in a different sense, as Romeo does with Benvolio's "hit" using it in the sense as "guess." There are many metaphors from archery in Shakespeare and in Elizabethan literature in general.

207. "Dian's wit": the good sense of Diana, Roman goddess of chastity.

210. "stay the siege of loving terms:" allow herself to be besieged with expression of love.

211. "assailing": i.e., with looks of love.

214. "her store": i.e., her store of wealth which consists of her beauty. She will leave no beauty behind her in her offspring. This is a continual thought in Shakespeare's sonnets.

220. "merit bliss": deserve the blessings of chastity.

221. "forsworn to": sworn not to.

222. "live dead": so do we talk of a "living death" (Oxymoron).

223. "ruled": advised.

224. "how . . . think": i.e., he can think of nothing else.

ROMEO AND JULIET

ACT I SCENE I

ACT I SCENE II

The setting is a street in Verona. Paris, a young nobleman who is related to Prince Escalus, is talking confidentially to Capulet. He tells Capulet that both he and Montague are honorable men, and should be able to keep the peace. But what Paris really wishes to know is whether Capulet will give him permission to marry his young daughter, Juliet, who is thirteen years of age. You will probably be surprised at her youth, but certain girls mature early and Juliet was one of these. She was strikingly beautiful, but did not want to consider marriage for a few years. Capulet explains that his daughter is "yet a stranger in the world," and says she should wait at least two more years before she grows "ripe to be a bride."

Paris replies that "Younger than she are happy mothers made," which may, or may not, be true. Mothers, yes; happy mothers, less certain. Capulet says that they are too soon spoiled, when they marry so early. He has great hopes for his young daughter, and does not wish to push her into a marriage at this stage in her development. However, he lets Paris woo her, to win her affections. If she agrees to marry Paris, Capulet will give his consent.

Capulet is giving a feast or masquerade that evening, to which he has invited many guests. He wishes Paris to attend, so that the young nobleman may have the opportunity to see Juliet and get to know her better.

Capulet gives his servant the list of guests, and tells him to "trudge about" through Verona inviting the people whose names are on the list to attend the feast at his home that evening.

After Capulet and Paris have gone out, the servant makes a short and amusing speech in which he says that he has to find those

---

Being black puts us in mind they hide the fair.
He that is strucken blind cannot forget
The precious treasure of his eyesight lost.   231
Show me a mistress that is passing fair,
What doth her beauty serve but as a note   233
Where I may read who passed that passing fair?   234
Farewell. Thou canst not teach me to forget.

Benvolio. I'll pay that doctrine, or else die in debt.   236
[*Exeunt.*

Scene two.

(THE SAME. A STREET)

Enter CAPULET, COUNTY PARIS, *the* Clown *and a* Servant.

Capulet. But Montague is bound as well as I,   1
In penalty alike; and 'tis not hard, I think,
For men so old as we to keep the peace.

Paris. Of honorable reckoning are you both,   4
And pity 'tis you lived at odds so long.   5
But now, my lord, what say you to my suit?

Capulet. But saying o'er what I have said before:
My child is yet a stranger in the world,
She hath not seen the change of fourteen years;   9
Let two more summers wither in their pride   10
Ere we may think her ripe to be a bride.

Paris. Younger than she are happy mothers made.

Capulet. And too soon marred are those so early made.   13
The earth hath swallowed all my hopes but she;   14
She is the hopeful lady of my earth.   15
But woo her, gentle Paris, get her heart;
My will to her consent is but a part.   17
An she agree, within her scope of choice
Lies my consent and fair according voice.   19
This night I hold an old accustomed feast,
Whereto I have invited many a guest,
Such as I love; and you among the store,
One more, most welcome, makes my number more.
At my poor house look to behold this night
Earth-treading stars that make dark heaven light.   25
Such comfort as do lusty young men feel
When well-apparelled April on the heel   27
Of limping Winter treads, even such delight   28
Among fresh fennel buds shall you this night
Inherit at my house. Hear all, all see,
And like her most whose merit most shall be;
Which, on more view of many, mine, being one,   32
May stand in number, though in reck'ning none.
Come, go with me. [*to* Servant, *giving him a paper*]
    Go, sirrah, trudge about   34
Through fair Verona; find those persons out
Whose names are written there, and to them say,
My house and welcome on their pleasure stay.
[*Exit, with* PARIS.

Servant. Find them out whose names are written

---

231. "his eyesight": what he saw once.

233. "note": memorandum.

234. "passed": surpassed (in the same sense as "passing," above).

236. "I'll pay that doctrine": i.e., I will pay you back in your own coin and show you that you cannot teach me to forget (to try to make you forget). Romeo says that Benvolio cannot teach him to forget, and in effect Benvolio says that he will have a good try.

---

1. "bound": bound over to keep the peace.

4. "reckoning": In view of Capulet's speech and the following line in Paris' speech, it would seem that Paris refers to the reckoning of their years, i.e., experience of life, not to their reputation in general.

5. "odds": enmity.

9. "change": she is not fully fourteen.

10. "wither in their pride": i.e., let their beautiful flowers wither. So do we talk of "the pride of summer."

13. "marred . . . made": a thoroughly Shakespearean antithesis. There is an undoubted reference to the proverb. "Soon married, soon marred."

14. "earth . . . hopes": i.e., all my (other) children are dead and buried.

15. "earth": i.e., body, offspring. Capulet may mean that his daughter is the heiress of his land, but it seems not so likely as in this speech Capulet's mind is not on material things.

17. "My will . . . part": my permission follows on (is but a part of) her choice.

19. "fair according": agreeing willingly.

25. "Earth-treading": stars that make dark heaven light—beauties are like stars come down to earth, sending rays of light upwards . . .

27. "well-apparelled": bringing foliage to clothe the trees.

28. "limping": slowly retreating.

32. "Which . . . none": this is differently punctuated in different editions, giving two different meanings. (1) When you have seen more of her whose merit is most (the antecedent of "which"), many—including my daughter—may be in the company, but none may be reckoned with her. (2) When you have seen many ladies, my daughter being one, she may be one of the company, but not one for whom you have any esteem. (1) has a comma at "of," and (2) at "many." The first seems more in character, in view of Capulet's words about what his daughter means to him, but if the second be accepted it could be said that he wants to save this daughter from an unhappy marriage, and make sure that Paris' mind is made up and that his affection is not a passing fancy.

34. "sirrah": a familiar (or contemptuous) form of "sir," generally used when speaking to inferiors.

ROMEO AND JULIET

ACT I SCENE II

persons whose names are here written down; unfortunately, he does not know how to read and must go to the "learned" for help.

Benvolio enters, with Romeo. Benvolio tells Romeo that he should find a new interest to outgrow his passionate obsession with this cruel sweetheart, but Romeo answers in such strange fashion that his friend asks him if he is mad.

Capulet's servant enters and asks Romeo if he can read. The servant needs to have the guest list read out to him, but Romeo answers strangely so the servant wonders whether Romeo, too, is illiterate. Romeo volunteers to read the list, and does so (while the servant listens carefully, remembering all the names in order). The servant reveals that the feast is being given by his master, "the great rich Capulet," and he adds "and if you be not of the house of Montagues, I pray, come and crush a cup of wine." Romeo has observed the name of a girl, Rosaline, on the guest list, and Benvolio reminds him that Romeo used to love her, and urges him to attend. She will soon drive out all other thoughts from Romeo's mind. Romeo, of course, does not agree; but he consents to go to the feast, though he doubts whether it will help him much.

The dramatic purposes of Scene II are:

1. It announces the Prince's decision concerning the disciplining of Capulet and Montague.

2. It introduces Paris as a proper suitor for Juliet.

3. It shows Capulet as a talkative matchmaker, anxious to please the Prince by yielding to Paris's demand to marry Juliet.

4. It provides a possible solution for Romeo's melancholy moodiness.

5. The servant's difficulties furnish the audience with comedy and amusement.

Note that the servant speaks entirely in prose, as befits his menial status; Capulet, Paris, Benvolio, and Romeo employ iambic pentameter, with the occasional use of sextains (e.g. by Benvolio, before the meeting with the servant; and by Romeo after the servant's departure).

here? It is written that the shoemaker should meddle with his yard and the tailor with his last, the fisher with his pencil and the painter with his nets; but I am sent to find those persons whose names are here writ, and can never find what names the writing person hath here writ. I must to the learned. In good time! 44

Enter BENVOLIO *and* ROMEO.

Benvolio. Tut, man, one fire burns out another's 45
  burning;
  One pain is less'ned by another's anguish;
Turn giddy, and be holp by backward turning; 47
  One desperate grief cures with another's languish. 48
Take thou some new infection to thy eye,
And the rank poison of the old will die.
Romeo. Your plantain leaf is excellent for that. 51
Benvolio. For what, I pray thee?
Romeo.   For your broken shin.
Benvolio. Why, Romeo, art thou mad?
Romeo. Not mad, but bound more than a madman is;
Shut up in prison, kept without my food,
Whipped and tormented and—God-den, good fellow. 56
Servant. God gi' go-den. I pray, sir, can you read? 57
Romeo. Ay, mine own fortune in my misery.
Servant. Perhaps you have learned it without book. But I pray, can you read anything you see?
Romeo. Ay, if I know the letters and the language.
Servant. Ye say honestly. Rest you merry. 62
Romeo. Stay, fellow; I can read.
                   [He reads the letter.
'Signior Martino and his wife and daughters;
County Anselmo and his beauteous sisters; 65
The lady widow of Vitruvio;
Signior Placentio and his lovely nieces;
Mercutio and his brother Valentine;
Mine uncle Capulet, his wife, and daughters;
My fair niece Rosaline and Livia; 70
Signior Valentio and his cousin Tybalt;
Lucio and the lively Helena.'
A fair assembly. Whither should they come?
Servant. Up.
Romeo. Whither? To supper?
Servant. To our house.
Romeo. Whose house?
Servant. My master's.
Romeo. Indeed I should have asked you that before.
Servant. Now I'll tell you without asking. My master is the great rich Capulet; and if you be not of the house of Montagues, I pray come and crush a cup of 82
wine. Rest you merry.   *[Exit.*
Benvolio. At this same ancient feast of Capulet's 84
Sups the fair Rosaline whom thou so loves;
With all the admired beauties of Verona.
Go thither, and with unattainted eye
Compare her face with some that I shall show,
And I will make thee think thy swan a crow.
Romeo. When the devout religion of mine eye 90
  Maintains such falsehood, then turn tears to fires;
And these, who, often drowned, could never die, 92
  Transparent heretics, be burnt for liars!
One fairer than my love? The all-seeing sun

39-41. The servant's confusion is deliberately contrived by Shakespeare: thus,
"shoemaker . . .": last,
"tailor . . .": yard,
"fisher . . .": nets,
"painter . . .": pencil.

44. "I must to the learned": must go to someone who can read.

45. "one fire burns out another's burning": i.e., a greater fire soon burns up the material of a lesser, or Benvolio may be referring to the country superstition that the sun puts out a fire in a grate.

47. "holp": archaic form of helped.

48. "cures with another's languish": on the parallel of the "pain" this would mean "is cured when another (grief) brings a depressing effect."

51. "Your plantain leaf": a dock-leaf. Romeo means that a dock-leaf is useful for minor ills—to stop bleeding from a scratch, for instance—but his ailment needs a more desperate remedy.

56. "God-den": good evening, a contraction of the fuller "God give you a good even."

57. "gi' ": give (you).

62. "Rest you merry": a colloquial term of farewell, comparable to our "All the best!"

65. "County": another form of "count," not infrequently used by Shakespeare.

70. "Rosaline": the first time Romeo's lady-love is named.

82. "crush a cup": a common colloquial expression in Elizabethan English comparable to "crack a bottle."

84. "ancient": one which has been held annually for a long time.

90. "devout religion": implying that he worships Rosaline.

92. "these": i.e., these eyes of mine "drown'd" in tears).

ACT I SCENE III

The setting is a room in Capulet's magnificent house in Verona. Lady Capulet is alone with the aged crone who nurses Capulet's thirteen-year-old daughter, Juliet. Lady Capulet tells the nurse to call Juliet, who soon arrives. Her entrance is one that we have been awaiting expectantly, for Juliet's beauty has already reached us from two sources at least. She is small, delicate, radiant, and has an exquisite speaking voice. Her mother wishes to speak with her, privately, so the old nurse is told to leave them alone. Then Lady Capulet recalls that the nurse knows all their secrets, so she calls her back again. She again makes the point that Juliet is not yet fourteen.

The language of the nurse is coarse, and, sometimes, bawdy. She is a comic creation, and has something of the procuress in her nature. She cracks jokes that might be thought to be in bad taste by a few people, but she is an old and trusted servant of a former era, and we must not be too moralistic in judging what she says.

In just over two weeks Juliet will be fourteen. The nurse has looked after Juliet since the child's birth, and recalls acting as the child's wet-nurse before she was weaned. The nurse also recalls various incidents of Juliet's infancy and early childhood. Her husband, who was a merry fellow, once picked up the child and asked her if she fell on her face. "Thou wilt fall backward when thou hast more wit; wilt thou not, Jule?" he told her, with crude though natural foresight. His vulgarity must have paralleled that of his wife when he lived. Lady Capulet tells her to hold her peace. The old nurse cannot do this, and tells her sordid story for the second time using exactly the same words.

Lady Capulet confesses that she has come to talk of Juliet's marriage. This is an "honour" (the word is used ironically) that Juliet did

---

Ne'er saw her match since first the world begun.
Benvolio. Tut! you saw her fair, none else being by,
Herself poised with herself in either eye;　97
But in that crystal scales let there be weighed　98
Your lady's love against some other maid　99
That I will show you shining at this feast,
And she shall scant show well that now seems best.　101
Romeo. I'll go along, no such sight to be shown,
But to rejoice in splendor of my own.　[*Exeunt.* 103

Scene three.

(A ROOM IN CAPULET'S HOUSE.)

Enter CAPULET'S Wife, *and* Nurse.

Wife. Nurse, where's my daughter? Call her forth
　to me.
Nurse. Now, by my maidenhead at twelve year old,　2
I bade her come. What, lamb! what, ladybird!　3
God forbid, where's this girl? What, Juliet!　4

Enter JULIET.

Juliet. How now? Who calls?
Nurse.　　　　　　　Your mother.
Juliet.　　　　　　　Madam, I am here.
What is your will?
Wife. This is the matter—Nurse, give leave awhile,
We must talk in secret. Nurse, come back again;
I have remem'red me, thou 's here our counsel.　9
Thou knowest my daughter's of a pretty age.　10
Nurse. Faith, I can tell her age unto an hour.
Wife. She's not fourteen.
Nurse.　　　　　I'll lay fourteen of my teeth—
And yet, to my teen be it spoken, I have but four —
She's not fourteen. How long is it now
To Lammastide?　15
Wife.　　　　A fortnight and odd days.
Nurse. Even or odd, of all days in the year.
Come Lammas Eve at night shall she be fourteen.
Susan and she (God rest all Christian souls!)
Were of an age. Well, Susan is with God;
She was too good for me. But, as I said,
On Lammas Eve at night shall she be fourteen;
That shall she, marry; I remember it well.　22
'Tis since the earthquake now eleven years;　23
And she was weaned (I never shall forget it),
Of all the days of the year, upon that day;
For I had then laid wormwood to my dug,　26
Sitting in the sun under the dovehouse wall.
My lord and you were then at Mantua.
Nay, I do bear a brain. But, as I said,　29
When it did taste the wormwood on the nipple
Of my dug and felt it bitter, pretty fool,　31
To see it tetchy and fall out with the dug!　32
Shake, quoth the dovehouse! 'Twas no need, I trow,　33
To bid me trudge.　34
And since that time it is eleven years,
For then she could stand high-lone; nay, by th' rood,　36

---

97. "either eye": i.e., in each of your eyes.

98. "scales": Romeo's eyes.

99. "lady's love": love for your lady. To interpret "the slight love of your lady for you" shifts the emphasis and is unlikely.

101. "scant show well": scarcely appear attractive.

103. "splendor of mine own": the splendid beauty of my own beloved.

2. "maidenhead": virginity.

3. "ladybird": a term of endearment, similar to "lamb."

4. "God forbid": that Juliet should be harmed.

9. "remem'red me": the "me" can be ignored. Actually it is a reflexive use, lit. "reminded myself." "thou's": thou shalt. The Elizabethan use of "thou" and "you" is clearly shown in this conversation. "Thou" was a sign of familiarity, "you" was a formal address used by servant to master.
Compare also the conversation between Sampson and Gregory in the first scene; also that between Tybalt and Benvolio which follows (where Tybalt uses the second person contemptuously, as towards an inferior) and that between Montague and Benvolio after Romeo's entrance (though previously Montague had addressed his nephew as "you").

10. "pretty": marriageable, ripe for marriage.

15. "Lammastide": Lammas or Loaf Mass day (1 August) was a festival for the hallowing of bread.

22. "marry": I swear (literally by Mary).

23. "since the earthquake": there was an earthquake in England in 1580, and a bad one in Verona in 1570. Some have taken the reference to be to the 1580 earthquake and have deduced therefrom that the date of the writing of the play was 1591, but the garrulous old Nurse is not one whose memory is to be trusted.

26. "wormwood": a plant with a bitter juice to make the child stop drinking (foster-) mother's milk.

29. "do bear a brain": have a retentive memory.

31. "fool": a term of endearment—darling or innocent.

32. "tetchy": fretful, peevish.

33. "Shake, quoth the dovehouse": the dovehouse began shaking—a colloquial use of "quoth" still occasionally found in small rural communities of Warwickshire.

34. "trudge": walk away.

36. "high-lone": quite alone.
"rood": cross (of Christ).

ROMEO AND JULIET

ACT I SCENE III

not expect to receive so soon. The nurse misunderstands Juliet's use of the term "honour" to describe her marriage, and assumes Juliet means it literally. This pleases the nurse, but probably annoys Juliet.

Lady Capulet tells Juliet that many girls marry young, and that she herself was married when she was about Juliet's own age. Then she bluntly tells her that the brave Paris is asking for her hand.

The nurse is delighted that "a man," especially a "man of war" such as Paris, is all set to woo Juliet. Mother and nurse praise the young nobleman's virtues, and Lady Capulet asks Juliet whether she can love this young man, even before she mentions that he will be present at the feast at their house that evening. She asks for a brief answer, but Juliet does not commit herself to a positive reply. She does agree, however, to look to like him, "if looking liking move."

A servant enters and announces that the guests are there, and supper is about to be served. The two ladies have been asked to go downstairs, the nurse has been cursed in the pantry by the other servants, and everything is in "extremity." He goes out rather distractedly, beseeching the ladies to follow straight. These large gatherings were very hard on the servants who did all the work for them!

The women leave, Lady Capulet urging the Count Paris on her daughter, and the nurse calling out a suggestive remark about happy nights and happy days.

The dramatic purposes of Scene III are:

1. To introduce Juliet as an unspoiled, innocent, charming, submissive, and passionate normal girl.

2. To show the audience what the Capulet domestic atmosphere is like.

3. To develop the characters of Lady Capulet, and the Nurse —who is one of the most interesting persons in the play, with her earthy humor and delight in disconnected biographical reminiscence.

4. To show the purpose of the masquerade, so that the audience is suitably prepared for it—and for what follows.

She could have run and waddled all about;
For even the day before, she broke her brow; 38
And then my husband (God be with his soul!
'A was a merry man) took up the child.
'Yea,' quoth he, 'dost thou fall upon thy face?
Thou wilt fall backward when thou hast more wit;
Wilt thou not, Jule?' and, by my holidam, 43
The pretty wretch left crying and said 'Ay.'
To see now how a jest shall come about!
I warrant, an I should live a thousand years,
I never should forget it. 'Wilt thou not, Jule?' quoth he,
And, pretty fool, it stinted and said 'Ay.'
Wife. Enough of this. I pray thee hold thy peace.
Nurse. Yes, madam. Yet I cannot choose but laugh
To think it should leave crying and say 'Ay.'
And yet, I warrant, it had upon it brow
A bump as big as a young cock'rel's stone;
A perilous knock; and it cried bitterly.
'Yea,' quoth my husband, 'fall'st upon thy face?
Thou wilt fall backward when thou comest to age;
Wilt thou not, Jule?' It stinted and said 'Ay.'
Juliet. And stint thou too, I pray thee, nurse, say I.
Nurse. Peace, I have done. God mark thee to his grace;
Thou wast the prettiest babe that e'er I nursed.
An I might live to see thee married once, 61
I have my wish.
Wife. Marry, that 'marry' is the very theme 63
I came to talk of. Tell me, daughter Juliet,
How stands your disposition to be married?
Juliet. It is an honor that I dream not of.
Nurse. An honor? Were not I thine only nurse, 67
I would say thou hadst sucked wisdom from thy teat. 68
Wife. Well, think of marriage now. Younger than you,
Here in Verona, ladies of esteem,
Are made already mothers. By my count,
I was your mother much upon these years
That you are now a maid. Thus then in brief:
The valiant Paris seeks you for his love.
Nurse. A man, young lady! lady, such a man
As all the world—why he's a man of wax. 76
Wife. Verona's summer hath not such a flower.
Nurse. Nay, he's a flower, in faith—a very flower.
Wife. What say you? Can you love the gentleman?
This night you shall behold him at our feast.
Read o'er the volume of young Paris' face,
And find delight writ there with beauty's pen;
Examine every married lineament, 83
And see how one another lends content; 84
And what obscured in this fair volume lies
Find written in the margent of his eyes. 86
This precious book of love, this unbound lover, 87
To beautify him only lacks a cover. 88
The fish lives in the sea, and 'tis much pride
For fair without the fair within to hide. 90
That book in many's eyes doth share the glory,
That in gold clasps locks in the golden story; 92
So shall you share all that he doth possess,
By having him making yourself no less. 94
Nurse. No less? Nay, bigger! Women grow by men.
Wife. Speak briefly, can you like of Paris' love?

38. "broke her brow": cut her forehead.

43. "Jule": affectionate diminutive for Juliet.
"holidam": originally the holy relics upon which oaths were sworn; by the late sixteenth-century this word was used as a weak asseveration or mild oath.

61. "live . . . once": only live to see you married.

63. "Marry, that 'marry'": the first is a corruption of the oath "By Mary," the second is the verb to wed.

67. "Were not I thine only nurse": but since she is, to say so would be to praise herself.

68. "from thy teat": from me (the Nurse had been Juliet's wet-nurse).

76. "of wax": i.e., as handsome as if he had been modeled in wax, finer than men usually are.

83. "married": harmonious, symmetrical, well balanced.
"lineament": part or feature of a face, with attention to outline.

84. "one another lends content": one sets off another to advantage.

86. "margent": margin; the general sense is that what you cannot find written in his face you will find out in his eyes.

87. "unbound": unbounded, unmarried, free (pun on 'unbound' book).

88. "cover": the binding (bonds) of marriage.

90. "fair without . . . hide": i.e., for the beautiful sea to contain beautiful fish.

92. "That in . . . story": i.e., is beautiful to look at on the outside as well as having a beautiful story within. The application is that Paris has a fair appearance "outside" and a good character "within."

94. "making yourself no less": at the same time not lessening your own possessions.

ROMEO AND JULIET

ACT I SCENE III

ACT I SCENE IV

Benvolio rounds up the masquers, men who plan to attend a fancy dress ball or masquerade disguised in masks, an old Italian pastime. The group includes Mercutio, who is a high-spirited young man noted for his wit. Romeo early declares punningly that he "is not for this ambling; being but heavy," he says, "I will bear the light." Accompanied by five or six other Masquers, and some torch-bearers and, probably, drummers, they make their way up the main street of the city. They reach the front of Capulet's house, and wait for the dinner to end and the revelry to begin. While waiting, Romeo and Mercutio jest with one another, and Benvolio waits impatiently.

Shakespeare knew that at this time in England it was customary for uninvited masquers to arrive at a large party such as Capulet's, and announce their arrival in a brief speech. The host usually admitted them to the party. Romeo inquires about the speech of announcement, but Benvolio suggests they enter, dance, then leave without a speech.

Juliet. I'll look to like, if looking liking move;   97
But no more deep will I endart mine eye   98
Than your consent gives strength to make it fly.

Enter Servingman.

Servingman. Madam, the guests are come, supper served up, you called, my young lady asked for, the nurse cursed in the pantry, and everything in extremity. I must hence to wait. I beseech you follow straight.   102

Wife. We follow thee [*Exit* Servingman.] Juliet, the County stays.

Nurse. Go, girl, seek happy nights to happy days.
[*Exeunt.*

Scene four.

(THE SAME. A STREET)

Enter ROMEO, MERCUTIO, BENVOLIO, *with five or six other* Maskers; Torchbearers.

Romeo. What, shall this speech be spoke for our   1
excuse?
Or shall we on without apology?

Benvolio. The date is out of such prolixity.   3
We'll have no Cupid hoodwinked with a scarf,   4
Bearing a Tartar's painted bow of lath,   5
Scaring the ladies like a crowkeeper;   6
[Nor no without-book prologue, faintly spoke   7
After the prompter, for our entrance;]
But, let them measure us by what they will,
We'll measure them a measure and be gone.   10

Romeo. Give me a torch. I am not for this ambling.   11
Being but heavy, I will bear the light.   12

Mercutio. Nay, gentle Romeo, we must have you dance.

Romeo. Not I, believe me. You have dancing shoes
With nimble soles; I have a soul of lead
So stakes me to the ground I cannot move.

Mercutio. You are a lover. Borrow Cupid's wings
And soar with them above a common bound.

Romeo. I am too sore enpiercèd with his shaft
To soar with his light feathers; and so bound
I cannot bound a pitch above dull woe.   21
Under love's heavy burden do I sink.

Mercutio. And, to sink in it, should you burden   23
love—
Too great oppression for a tender thing.

Romeo. Is love a tender thing? It is too rough,
Too rude, too boist'rous, and it pricks like thorn.

Mercutio. If love be rough with you, be rough with love
Prick love for pricking, and you beat love down.   28
Give me a case to put my visage in.   29

97. "look to": expect to.
"looking liking move": what I see makes me like him. "Looking" is the subject of "move," "liking" the object.

98. "But no . . . fly": i.e., I will go no farther than you approve.

102. "extremity": a muddle.
"wait": i.e., upon the guests.

"maskers": men masked for a masquerade—a masked ball, not a masque, the elaborate entertainment which was coming into fashion among the nobility at the end of Shakespeare's career.

1. "this speech": i.e., speech of apology (for coming to the ball without a formal invitation) as the next line shows.

3. "The date is out": it is no longer the fashion.
"such prolixity": such long-winded verbosity.

4. "Cupid": a guest disguised as Cupid, as a spokesman to make their speech of apology.
"hoodwinked": blindfold (like a hawk).

5. "Tartar's painted bow of lath": i.e., an imitation (painted and of lath) of a Tartar bow such as Cupid is represented with.

6. "crowkeeper": boy acting as a scarecrow.

7. "Nor no": in Elizabethan English a double negative intensifies the idea instead of logically cancelling it.
"without-book": impromptu, or perhaps from memory.

10. "measure them a measure": dance a measure (a slow and stately dance)—punning on the word as used in the previous note.

11. "Give me a torch": i.e., I do not want to dance, so I will be one of the torch bearers.
"ambling": impolite term for rustic dancing.

12. "heavy . . . light": Romeo is rather fond of this punning antithesis. In I.I., he spoke of "heavy lightness," and Montague too said, "Away from light steals home my heavy son" (I.I.). "Heavy"—heavy of heart.

21. "pitch": a metaphor from falconry. The "pitch" was the technical word for the height to which a falcon soared before swooping on her prey.

23. "to sink in it, should you burden love": you would be too heavy a burden for love if you should sink in it.

28. "Prick love for pricking": i.e., give love back as good (or as bad) as it gives you, or in modern metaphor, pay it back in its own coin.

29. "case": mask (obsolete, masque) or visor.

ROMEO AND JULIET

ACT I SCENE IV

Romeo does not wish to participate except as an onlooker; Mercutio urges him to deal roughly with love, and calls for his visor (mask). Romeo still refuses to dance, and reveals that he has had a dream which seemed to indicate personal danger to him if he attends the dance.

Mercutio ridicules this dream and its interpretation, and, in the Queen Mab speech, imagines the queen of the fairies as a tiny mid-wife, or instigator of magical work. In this speech he describes Queen Mab's appearance and surroundings in considerable detail, and makes some very delicate poetic comparisons. Mercutio blames Queen Mab for the dreams people experience, and he interprets some of them in an exaggerated way. Benvolio interrupts this speech, annoyed at the delay, and anxious not to be late for the dance.

Romeo is now less unwilling to attend, but first expresses a presentiment that evil will follow. Benvolio orders the drums to beat, signaling their arrival.

The dramatic structure of this scene is not enhanced by the long unrhymed Queen Mab speech of the mercurial Mercutio, but this speech is remarkable owing to its play of fancy or imagination, its imagery, the exquisite texture of its language, and the cleverness of its composition. It sustains the suspense of the audience, and both parallels to and contrasts with the Nurse's story of Juliet in the preceding scene.

A visor for a visor! What care I	30
What curious eye doth quote deformities?	31
Here are the beetle brows shall blush for me.	32
Benvolio. Come, knock and enter; and no sooner in	
But every man betake him to his legs.	34
Romeo. A torch for me! Let wantons light of heart	
Tickle the senseless rushes with their heels;	
For I am proverbed with a grandsire phrase,	37
I'll be a candle-holder and look on;	
The game was ne'er so fair, and I am done.	39
Mercutio. Tut! dun's the mouse, the constable's own word!	40
If thou art Dun, we'll draw thee from the mire	41
Of this sir-reverence love, within thou stickest	42
Up to the ears. Come, we burn daylight, ho!	43
Romeo. Nay, that's not so.	
Mercutio. I mean, sir, in delay	
We waste our lights in vain, like lamps by day.	
Take our good meaning, for our judgment sits	
Five times in that ere once in our five wits.	47
Romeo. And we mean well in going to this masque,	
But 'tis no wit to go.	
Mercutio. Why, make one ask?	
Romeo. I dreamt a dream to-night.	49
Mercutio. And so did I.	
Romeo. Well, what was yours?	
Mercutio. That dreamers often lie.	
Romeo. In bed asleep, while they do dream things true,	
Mercutio. O, then I see Queen Mab hath been with you.	53
She is the fairies' midwife, and she comes	
In shape no bigger than an agate stone	55
On the forefinger of an alderman,	
Drawn with a team of little atomies	57
Over men's noses as they lie asleep;	
Her wagon spokes made of long spinners' legs,	59
The cover, of the wings of grasshoppers;	60
Her traces, of the smallest spider's web;	61
Her collars, of the moonshine's wat'ry beams;	62
Her whip, of cricket's bone; the lash, of film;	63
Her wagoner, a small grey-coated gnat,	64
Not half so big as a round little worm	
Pricked from the lazy finger of a maid;	66
Her chariot is an empty hazelnut,	
Made by the joiner squirrel or old grub,	68
Time out o' mind the fairies' coachmakers.	
And in this state she gallops by night	
Through lovers' brains, and then they dream of love;	
O'er courtiers' knees, that dream on curtsies straight;	
O'er lawyers' fingers, who straight dream on fees;	
O'er ladies' lips, who straight on kisses dream,	
Which oft the angry Mab with blisters plagues,	
Because their breaths with sweetmeats tainted are	76
Sometimes she gallops o'er a courtier's nose,	
And then dreams he of smelling out a suit;	

30. "A visor for a visor!": i.e., fancy putting a mask on my face, which is funny enough to be a mask by itself.

31. "quote" note carefully for future malicious use.

32. "Here . . . me": Mercutio means that he cares not what people think of him; if anyone blushes for him, it shall be himself.

34. "betake him to his legs": i.e., in dancing. We shall then, he infers, be lost in the crowd and less likely to be noticed.

37. "proverbed with a grandsire phrase": supported by an old man's proverb (that the candleholder, or looker-on, sees most of the game).

39. "The game . . . done": this is the best part of the proceedings, so I am giving up before worse comes. Another proverb, recommending people to give up while things are at their best, before the good impression is lost.

40. "dun's the mouse": a slang Elizabethan phrase meaning "Keep quiet," hence. "The constable's own word."

41. "If . . . mire": "Dun is in the mire" is an old country game. Dun was a log standing for a cart horse in the mire. In moving the log there was much fun and merriment, such as pushing one another down and trying to make the log fall on one another's toes.

42. "sir-reverence": filth, dung (a special form of "mire"). "Sir-reverence" came to mean this because the word prefaced mention of unpleasant things (a corruption of "save your reverence," i.e., excuse my mentioning it).

43. "we burn daylight": i.e., we are wasting time (from the burning of candles in daylight).

47. "in that": i.e., in our "good meaning." "five wits": i.e., being clever in playing with words.

49. "to-night": last night.

53. "Queen Mab": spoken of here as the Queen of the Fairies.

55. "agate stone": hard stone used for the engraved part of a seal ring.

57. "atomies": miniature beings.

59. "spinners'": spiders'.

60. "cover": i.e., hood of the "waggon."

61. "traces": joining the horses to the "waggon."

62. "collars": i.e., of the horses.

63. "film": gossamer thread, like that spun by a spider.

64. "wagoner": one who drives a waggon.

66. "lazy": because laziness was thought to induce such growths.

68. "old grub": the grub bores his way through nuts, as the squirrel cracks them. "joiner": carpenter (applied to the squirrel because of his chisel-sharp teeth).

76. "tainted": presumably because their breaths are not naturally sweet and they use flavored sweetmeats to smother the foulness.

ROMEO AND JULIET

ACT I SCENE IV

The dramatic purposes of this scene are:

1. To sustain the audience's suspense concerning the outcome of the masquerade.

2. To bring Romeo's love-lorn state before the audience once more.

3. To introduce the exotic Mercutio.

4. To prefigure future tragedy in the fears and sentiments of Romeo.

The whole scene is in unrhymed, or blank, verse, except for some incidental and almost accidental rhyme, e.g. lines 53, 54—true/you.

ACT I SCENE V

The dance is the event to which we, the audience, have been looking forward eagerly, because we sense that during it something fateful may happen. Tension is high throughout the scene, and the gaiety of the scene captivates both eye and ear. The ladies' renaissance Italian dresses combined with the dark, embroidered costumes of the gentlemen present a striking and colorful spectacle, which is enhanced by the music and dancing, the side quarreling and love-whispering, and the controlled, animated movement everywhere.

And sometime comes she with a tithe-pig's tail 79
Tickling a parson's nose as 'a lies asleep,
Then dreams he of another benefice.
Sometimes she driveth o'er a soldier's neck,
And then dreams he of cutting foreign throats,
Of breaches, ambuscadoes, Spanish blades, 84
Of healths five fathom deep; and then anon 85
Drums in his ear, at which he starts and wakes, 86
And being thus frighted, swears a prayer or two
And sleeps again. This is that very Mab
That plats the manes of horses in the night
And bakes the elflocks in foul sluttish hairs, 90
Which once untangled much misfortune bodes. 91
This is the hag, when maids lie on their backs,
That presses them and learns them first to bear,
Making them women of good carriage.
This is she—
  Romeo.   Peace, peace, Mercutio, peace!
Thou talk'st of nothing.
  Mercutio.   True, I talk of dreams;
Which are the children of an idle brain,
Begot of nothing but vain fantasy; 98
Which is as thin of substance as the air,
And more inconstant than the wind, who woos 100
Even now the frozen bosom of the North
And, being angered, puffs away from thence,
Turning his side to the dew-dropping South.
  Benvolio. This wind you talk of blows us from 104
    ourselves.
Supper is done, and we shall come too late.
  Romeo. I fear, too early; for my mind misgives
Some consequence, yet hanging in the stars,
Shall bitterly begin his fearful date 108
With this night's revels and expire the term
Of a despised life, closed in my breast,
By some vile forfeit of untimely death.
But he that hath the steerage of my course
Direct my sail! On, lusty gentlemen! 113
  Benvolio. Strike, drum. 114

Scene five.

(The Same. A Hall in Capulet's House)

They march about the stage, and Servingmen *come forth with napkins.*

1st Servingman. Where's Potpan, that he helps not to take away? He shift a trencher? he scrape a trencher! 2

2nd Servingman. When good manners shall lie all 4 in one or two men's hands, and they unwashed too, 'tis a foul thing.

1st Servingman. Away with the joint-stools, remove 6 the court-cupboard, look to the plate. Good thou, save 7 me a piece of marchpane and, as thou loves me, let 8 the porter let in Susan Grindstone and Nell. [*Exit*

2nd Servingman. Anthony, and Potpan!

---

79. "tithe-pig's": a pig given as a tithe (tenth part) to a church thus a payment of ecclesiastical tax.

84. "breaches": gaps made (by the attackers) in fortifications. "ambuscadoes": ambushes.

85. "anon": straight away, immediately, at once (lit. in one).

86. "Drums": the signal for battle.

90. "elflocks": when dirty hair became clotted together it was superstitiously put down to elves, hence "elflocks." It happened only to filthy hair, hence "foul sluttish hairs."

91. "untangled": entangled.

98. "fantasy": fancy.

100. "woos . . . North": i.e., blows warmly on the northern wastes.

104. "This wind you talk of": probably with the implication that Mercutio is a windbag.
"from ourselves": away from our purpose.

108. "date": season.

113. "lusty gentlemen": corresponding to "my fine fellows."

114. "Strike, drum": spoken to the drummer-boy, a sign that they shall march on.

2. "trencher": wooden plate, lit. one to cut food upon.

4. "When . . . hands": i.e., when only one or two men do their duty.

6. "joint-stools": folding stools (not all in one piece).

7. "court-cupboard": movable sideboard, on which the food was placed.
"plate": silver plate.

8. "marchpane": confectionery made of almond paste, sugar, and marzipan.

ROMEO AND JULIET

ACT I SCENE V

The servants (not including the reluctant—or lazy—Potpan) clear away the trestle tables and prepare the hall for dancing. Guests and masquers enter by different doors. Lord and Lady Capulet, with their daughter Juliet, follow—or lead—the guests into the hall. Capulet welcomes the masquers, invites them to dance, and jests about ladies who have no corns—afflictions no self-respecting women would admit having. Capulet gives the impression that he had been a successful lover in his youth—"could tell/A whispering tale in a fair lady's ear/Such as would please." Those days have gone, for him; but he orders the musicians to strike up, requests more light and less heat—though it is July, a fire burns in the grate (Shakespeare evidently has an English July rather than an Italian one in mind).

While Capulet reminisces with his ancient brother, Paris is dancing with Juliet, while Romeo looks on. Romeo inquires of a servant about Paris' partner, and learns her identity. His romantic excitement on first seeing Juliet breaks out spontaneously into lyric verse, and this "snowy dove," who puts the other women into the category of crows by comparison now becomes his prized objective. "O! she doth teach the torches to burn bright."

Tybalt recognizes Romeo's voice, that of a traditional enemy, and wishes to slay him on the spot. Tybalt's uncle, Capulet, commends Romeo's bearing and tells the unruly Tybalt that Romeo is "a virtuous and well-govern'd youth" in Verona. Tybalt refuses to be put off, and Capulet warns him: "this trick may chance to scathe you." Tybalt is ordered out of the house and leaves, threatening to revenge himself on Romeo.

Enter two more Servingmen.

3rd Servingman. Ay, boy, ready.

1st Servingman. You are looked for and called for, asked for and sought for, in the great chamber.

4th Servingman. We cannot be here and there too. Cheerily, boys! Be brisk awhile, and the longer liver 15 take all.

[*Exit third and fourth* Servingmen.

Enter CAPULET, *his* Wife, JULIET, TYBALT, Nurse, *and all the* Guests *and* Gentlewomen *to the* Maskers.

Capulet. Welcome, gentlemen! Ladies that have their toes

Unplagued with corns will walk a bout with you. 17
Ah ha, my mistress! which of you all
Will now deny to dance? She that makes dainty, 19
She I'll swear hath corns. Am I come near ye now? 20
Welcome, gentlemen! I have seen the day
That I have worn a visor and could tell
A whispering tale in a fair lady's ear,
Such as would please. 'Tis gone, 'tis gone, 'tis gone!
You are welcome, gentlemen! Come, musicians, play.

[*Music plays, and they dance.*

A hall, a hall! give room! and foot it, girls.
More light, you knaves! and turn the tables up, 27
And quench the fire, the room is grown too hot. 28
Ah, sirrah, this unlooked-for sport comes well.
Nay, sit, nay, sit, good cousin Capulet, 30
For you and I are past our dancing days.
How long is't now since last yourself and I
Were in a mask?

2nd Capulet.   By'r Lady, thirty years. 33

Capulet. What, man? 'Tis not so much, 'tis not so much;
'Tis since the nuptial of Lucentio,
Come Pentecost as quickly as it will, 36
Some five-and-twenty years, and then we masked.

2nd Capulet. 'Tis more, 'tis more. His son is elder, 38
sir;
His son is thirty.

Capulet.   Will you tell me that?
His son was but a ward two years ago.

Romeo. [*to a* Servingman] What lady's that, which
doth enrich the hand 41
Of yonder knight?

Servingman. I know not, sir.

Romeo. O, she doth teach the torches to burn bright!
It seems she hangs upon the cheek of night
As a rich jewel in an Ethiop's ear— 46
Beauty too rich for use, for earth too dear!
So shows a snowy dove trooping with crows
As yonder lady o'er her fellows shows. 49
The measure done, I'll watch her place of stand 50
And, touching hers, make blessed my rude hand 51
Did my heart love till now? Forswear it, sight! 52
For I ne'er saw true beauty till this night.

Tybalt. This, by his voice, should be a Montague.
Fetch me my rapier, boy. What, dares the slave
Come hither, covered with an antic face, 56
To fleer and scorn at our solemnity? 57
Now, by the stock and honor of my kin,

15. "the longer liver to take all": a proverb, meaning that he who lives longest will get the most.

17. "walk a bout": dance a round.

19. "makes dainty": comes shyly.

20. "come near ye": touched you on the raw—where it hurts.

27. "turn the tables up": pack away the trestles and boards that constituted the tables.

28. "quench the fire": Shakespeare here forgets that the play is supposed to take place in July (1.2.16).

30. "cousin Capulet": the 'Uncle Capulet' of the invitation (referred to in Act I, Scene 2, line 67).

33. "By'r Lady": by our Lady, i.e., the Virgin Mary.

36. "Pentecost": the feast of Whitsunday.

38. "His son is elder": his (Lucentio's) son is older.

41. "enrich the hand": i.e., by dancing with him, he holds her hand.

46. "Ethiop's": Negro, as used by Shakespeare (here and elsewhere), not Ethiopian in its narrower sense.

49. "fellows": i.e., fellow-dancers.

50. "place of stand": notice that in those days between dances, dancers stood up, as, indeed, people did in church, at parish meetings, etc.

51. "rude": common.

52. "sight": he appeals to his sight to foreswear his previous love on account of what follows in the next line.

56. "antic": grotesque mask.

57. "fleer": scorn, or smock at. "solemnity": ceremonial festival.

ROMEO AND JULIET

ACT I SCENE V

Meanwhile, Romeo has been introducing himself to Juliet, and courts her in a formal sonnet—which they speak alternately in three quartets and a rhymed couplet. As a sonnet these speeches are structured thus:

(OCTAVE)

Romeo:
If I profane with my unworthiest hand
This holy shrine the gentle sin is this;
My lips, two blushing pilgrims, ready stand
To smooth that rough touch with a tender kiss.

Juliet:
Good pilgrim, you do wrong your hand too much,
Which mannerly devotion shows in this;
For saints have hands that pilgrims' hands do touch,
And palm to palm is holy palmers' kiss.

To strike him dead I hold it not a sin.

Capulet. Why, how now, kinsman? Wherefore storm
    you so?

Tybalt. Uncle, this is a Montague, our foe;
A villain, that is thither come in spite
To scorn at our solemnity this night.

Capulet. Young Romeo is it?

Tybalt.   'Tis he, that villain Romeo.

Capulet. Content thee, gentle coz, let him alone.
'A bears him like a portly gentleman,   66
And, to say truth, Verona brags of him
To be a virtuous and well-governed youth.
I would not for the wealth of all this town
Here in my house do him disparagement.   70
Therefore be patient, take no note of him.   71
It is my will, the which if thou respect,
Show a fair presence and put off these frowns.
An ill-beseeming semblance for a feast.

Tybalt. It fits when such a villain is a guest.
I'll not endure him.

Capulet.   He shall be endured.
What, goodman boy! I say he shall. Go to!   77
Am I the master here, or you? Go to!   78
You'll not endure him. God shall mend my soul!   79
You'll make a mutiny among my guests!
You will set cock-a-hoop, you'll be the man!   81

Tybalt. Why, uncle, 'tis a shame.

Capulet.   Go to, go to!
You are a saucy boy. Is't so, indeed?
This trick may chance to scathe you, I know what.   84
You must contrary me! Marry, 'tis time—   85
Well said, my hearts!—You are   a princox—go!   86
Be quiet, or—More light, more light!—For shame!
I'll make you quiet; what!—Cheerly, my hearts!

Tybalt. Patience perforce with willful choler meet-
    ing.   89
Makes my flesh tremble in their different greetings.   90
I will withdraw; but this intrusion shall,   91
Now seeming sweet; convert to bitt'rest gall. [*Exit.*

Romeo. If I profane with my unworthiest hand   93
  This holy shrine, the gentle sin is this;   94
My lips, two blushing pilgrims, ready stand
  To smooth that rough touch with a tender kiss.

Juliet. Good pilgrim, you do wrong your hand too
much,
  Which mannerly devotion shows in this;
For saints have hands that pilgrims' hands do touch,
  And palm to palm is holy palmers' kiss.

Romeo. Have not saints lips, and holy palmers too?

Juliet. Ay, pilgrim, lips that they must use in prayer.

Romeo. O, then, dear saint, let lips do what hands
do!
  They pray; grant thou, lest faith turn to despair.

Juliet. Saints do not move, though grant for prayers'   105
sake.

Romeo. Then move not while my prayer's effect I   106
take.
Thus from my lips, by thine my sin is purged.
                   [*Kisses her.*

---

66. "bears him": carries himself.
"portly": dignified, honorable, of good carriage or bearing.

70. "disparagement": discourtesy.

71. "patient": calm. Capulet does not mean, "Wait patiently for another opportunity."

77. "goodman boy": my fine fellow— with the implication in "boy" that he is only an underling after all.

78. "Go to": stop it, behave yourself.

79. "God . . . soul": an oath meaning 'God spare me if I will permit this!'

81. "set cock-a-hoop": orig.—to drink without stint, make good cheer recklessly, (hence) to cast off all restraint, give the rein to disorder, set all by the ears!

84. "This trick may chance to scathe you": I'll use this as an opportunity to injure you.
"what": Capulet is obviously hinting that if Tybalt's behavior does not improve he will find that it will affect his income, or his legacy in Capulet's will.

85. "contrary me": go against my will.

86. "hearts": good fellows. The rest of this speech is interspersed with remarks to the guests.
"princox": PRIN/ce of COX/combs; pert, saucy boy, upstart.

89. "Patience perforce": compulsory (enforced) patience.
"choler": anger.

90. "their different greeting": meeting of opposites.

91. "intrusion": i.e., of Romeo.

93. "hand": Romeo takes her hand as he says this. The next few speeches are in the form of a Shakespearean sonnet. Notice that the recurrence of the rhyming words "this" and "kiss" in Scene 2. 6 and 8 has a binding effect on the two quatrains of the octave, counteracting the separating influence of their being spoken by different people. It is significant that the first words between Romeo and Juliet are in sonnet form, as the sonnet was the accepted form for the language of love.

94. "This holy shrine": Juliet's body.

105. "move": alter, stir from what they know to be right.
"though grant": though they answer prayers.

106. "my prayer's effect": what is granted in answer to my prayer.

ROMEO AND JULIET

ACT I SCENE V

The introductory part, or thesis, is slow, courteous, cavalier, and passionate, in the tradition of Renaissance love poetry; Juliet's reply forms an appropriate antithesis. The contrasting, rapid, line-by-line interplay of verse parallels the heightening physical love play, and leads up to the sonnet climax, which ends in one extraneous line followed by a gentle, impassioned and prolonged kiss. It is the perfect correspondence of feeling and form which gives so much artistic pleasure to the audience in this part of the scene.

Notice the modesty of Juliet's terms: Romeo may kiss her, but she will not return the kiss. This is fully in keeping with the traditional, passive role of ladies for whom it was proper to be wooed, but for whom any active display of passion too early in a relationship was unseemly. (It was only much later, when 'ladies' had become 'women,' that they could respond actively to love,—thanks partly to the liberating effects of the teachings of Freud and D. H. Lawrence, and to the new understanding, knowledge, and acceptance, of the basic facts concerning human needs both emotional and biological).

Lady Capulet and the Nurse watch this romantic encounter with alarm; Juliet asks the Nurse who the young man is, and learns that he is a member of the rival family. "My only love sprung from my only hate," she laments, after declaring "My grave is like to be my wedding bed"—if Romeo should be already betrothed.

The dramatic purposes of this scene are:

1. It provides a visually satisfying spectacle, the masquerade containing gaiety, a quarrel, music, dancing, love scene, beautiful dresses and costumes, skillful contrasts of mood, suspense, and complex characterization.

2. It introduces the Renassiance hero, Romeo, to the Renaissance heroine, Juliet, in a singularly harmonious manner, by means of the sonnet interchange.

3. It adumbrates, or foreshadows, tragedy for Romeo and, therefore, for Juliet, through the alienation and aggrievement of Tybalt.

4. It adds to the development of the characters of Capulet and Romeo, and introduces both the gentle Juliet and the unruly and barbaric Tybalt.

Juliet. Then have my lips the sin that they have took.
Romeo. Sin from my lips? O trespass sweetly urged! 109
    Give me my sin again   [*Kisses her.*
Juliet.   You kiss by th' book. 111
Nurse. Madam, your mother craves a word with you.
Romeo. What is her mother? 113
Nurse.   Marry, bachelor,
Her mother is the lady of the house,
And a good lady, and a wise and virtuous.
I nursed her daughter that you talked withal.
I tell you, he that can lay hold of her
Shall have the chinks. 118
Romeo.   Is she a Capulet?
O dear account! my life is my foe's debt. 119
Benvolio. Away, be gone; the sport is at the best. 120
Romeo. Ay, so I fear; the more is my unrest. 121
Capulet. Nay, gentlemen, prepare not to be gone;
We have a trifling foolish banquet towards. 123
Is it e'en so? Why then, I thank you all. 124
I thank you, honest gentlemen. Good night.
More torches here! Come on then, let's to bed.
Ah, sirrah, by my fay, it waxes late; 127
I'll to my rest.   [*Exeunt all but* JULIET *and* Nurse.
Juliet. Come hither, nurse. What is yond gentleman?
Nurse. The son and heir of old Tiberio.
Juliet. What's he that now is going out of door?
Nurse. Marry, that, I think, be young Petruchio.
Juliet. What's he that follows there, that would not dance?
Nurse. I know not.
Juliet. Go ask his name.—If he be married,
My grave is like to be my wedding bed. 136
Nurse. His name is Romeo, and a Montague,
The only son of your great enemy.
Juliet. My only love, sprung from my only hate!
Too early seen unknown. and unknown too late! 140
Prodigious birth of love it is to me 141
That I must love a loathed enemy.
Nurse. What's this? what's this?
Juliet.   A rhyme I learnt even now
Of one I danced withal.   [*One calls within, 'Juliet.'*
Nurse.   Anon, anon!
Come, let's away; the strangers all are gone.
                           [*Exeunt.*

109. "trespass": i.e., accusation of sin.

111. "kiss by th' book": kiss according to the rules and techniques described by the erotic books, which reduce the art to a science.

113. "What": i.e., what position does she hold, what is her family and title. "Marry": an exclamation based on the oath, By Mary.

118. "chinks": cash (from the clatter of the coins).

119. "dear account": sad reckoning. In Elizabethan English the word "dear" intensified the meaning—you could have a "dear friend" and a "dear enemy." "my foe's debt": at the mercy of my foe (because he loves his foe).

120. "the sport is at the best": we have had the best of the fun.

121. "the more is my unrest": realizing what dangers there are in this sudden love for Juliet, Romeo applies Benvolio's comment to his own affairs.

123. "towards": coming, at hand.

124. "Is it e'en so": corresponding to our, "Must you really go?"

127. "fay": faith. "waxes": grows.

136. "My grave . . . bed": i.e., I am not likely to marry anyone else.

140. "too late": i.e., to make any difference—I cannot help loving him.

141. "Prodigious . . . enemy": (the fate) that I must love a loathed enemy is the portentous birth that love has given to me.

ROMEO AND JULIET

Like Act I, Act II opens with a Prologue meant to be recited by a chorus of voices but usually spoken by a single narrator in today's productions, when it is not omitted. This Prologue adds little of interest to the action of the play, and impedes rather than speeds the flow. For this and other reasons, this Prologue is frequently regarded as an insertion from the pen of a different writer, but it is unprofitable to haggle over this. The Prologue merely points out in a condensed way what has already taken place: Romeo has replaced an infatuation by a true love; his love is returned, but both lovers realize the perils of their attachment to one another; Romeo cannot have free access to Juliet since their families are antagonistic to each other; for the same reason, she cannot without difficulty arrange to meet him; nevertheless, "passion lends them power, time means, to meet"—and the dangers overcome make their meetings extremely sweet.

ACT II SCENE I

In a lane by the wall of Capulet's orchard (Anglo-Saxon wyrtgeart = plant-yard)—an interesting mixture of Stratford-upon-Avon and Verona?—Romeo is searching for the lovely girl he had met a few hours previously at the masquerade. Benvolio and Mercutio trace him to the foot of the orchard wall, but are unaware of his meeting with Juliet previously. They know he is hiding from them, and half good naturedly decide to leave him there, "consorted with the humorous night."

This scene has the following dramatic purposes:

1. It reveals the turmoil into which Romeo's new love has thrown him, as well as the unawareness of his friends at the new turn of romantic events, so fraught with consequences.

2. It develops the character of Mercutio, thereby preparing us for his increased importance later in the play.

3. It whets our appetites for the second meeting of the "star-crossed" lovers.

4. It acts as a brief interlude in which all may catch their breath before the piling-on of the following action.

THE PROLOGUE

Enter Chorus.

Chorus. Now old desire doth in his deathbed lie, 1
    And young affection gapes to be his heir; 2
That fair for which love groaned for and would die, 3
    With tender Juliet matched, is now not fair.
Now Romeo is beloved and loves again,
    Alike bewitched by the charm of looks; 6
But to his foe supposed he must complain, 7
    And she steal love's sweet bait from fearful hooks.
Being held a foe, he may not have access
    To breathe such vows as lovers use to swear, 10
And she as much in love, her means much less
    To meet her new beloved anywhere;
But passion lends them power, time means, to meet, 13
Temp'ring extremities with extreme sweet. [*Exit.* 14

ACT TWO, *scene one.*

(VERONA. A LANE BY THE WALL OF CAPULET'S ORCHARD)

Enter ROMEO *alone.*

Romeo. Can I go forward when my heart is here?
Turn back, dull earth, and find thy centre out. 2
    Enter BENVOLIO *with* MERCUTIO. ROMEO *retires.*
Benvolio. Romeo! my cousin Romeo! Romeo!
Mercutio.   He is wise,
And, on my life, hath stol'n him home to bed.
Benvolio. He ran this way and leapt this orchard wall.
Call, good Mercutio.
Mercutio.   Nay, I'll conjure too.
Romeo! humors! madman! passion! lover! 7
Appear thou in the likeness of a sigh!
Speak but one rhyme, and I am satisfied!
Cry but 'Ay me!' pronounce but 'love' and 'dove';
Speak to my gossip Venus one fair word, 11
One nickname for her purblind son and heir 12
Young Abraham Cupid, he that shot so true 13
When King Cophetua loved the beggar maid! 14
He heareth not, he stirreth not, he moveth not;
The ape is dead, and I must conjure him. 16
I conjure thee by Rosaline's bright eyes, 17
By her high forehead and her scarlet lip,
By her fine foot, straight leg, and quivering thigh,
And the demesnes that there adjacent lie, 20
That in thy likeness thou appear to us!
Benvolio. An if he hear thee, thou wilt anger him.
Mercutio. This cannot anger him, 'Twould anger him
    him
To raise a spirit in his mistress' circle
Of some strange nature, letting it there stand
Till she had laid it and conjured it down.

32

---

1. "old desire": Romeo's previous love, for Rosaline.

2. "young affection": Romeo's fresh love, for Juliet. "gapes": is keen.

3. "That fair" (one): Rosaline.

6. "Alike bewitched": each of them is equally enchanted.

7. "foe supposed": Juliet, who, as a member of the rival house, would normally be regarded as an enemy.

10. "use": are in the habit of.

13. "time": (lend them the) means.

14. "Temp'ring extremities": making their difficult positions easier by the sweetness of their meeting.

2. "earth": body.

7. "humors": evil moods.

11. "gossip" (Venus): friend (goddess of love).

12. "purblind": quite blind or merely dimsighted.

13. "Abraham Cupid": this expression has not been satisfactorily explained by any commentator, but may be an allusion to a famous archer of the day.

14. "King Cophetua": the story was a favorite ballad topic. Cupid shot "so trim" to bring about so unlikely an occurrence.

16. "ape": poor fellow.

17. "conjure": solemnly appeal to.

20. "demesnes": domains (of pleasure).

ACT II SCENE II

This scene, in which the celebrated second meeting of the young lovers takes place, is among the most romantic in English literature, and deserves a special place in the dramatic love poetry of the world. With its pathetic fallacy, in which the "fair sun" is invited to "kill the envious moon, who is already sick and pale with grief," its flights of poetic imagination, its splendid and moving love passages, and the lingering delays of parting, it and many of its linear components have become proverbial.

Romeo must have heard Mercutio calling to him in the previous scene, for he completes the Mercutio line ending with 'found' with a line ending in 'wound'—thereby making a rhymed couplet. The Elizabethans pronounced wound to rhyme with found—as we still pronounce the past participle of the verb 'to wind,' 'wound.'

Romeo approaches the Capulet house, gazes up at the windows, sees Juliet, while remaining unseen, and watches her look, cheek on hand, at the stars. Comparing her with the sun, he says she excels the moon. He implores Juliet not to follow the cold and chaste Diana, but to remain free to marry. In line 11 he breaks off to listen, yet Juliet only sighs and says nothing. Eventually, still unaware of Romeo's presence below, she breathes his name aloud. She refers to the obstacle of their families' feud, but concludes that a man's name mean little—it is his soul that counts. She invites him to "put off that name and take" her "in its place!"

That were some spite; my invocation
Is fair and honest: in his mistress' name,
I conjure only but to raise up him.
  Benvolio. Come, he hath hid himself among these trees
To be consorted with the humorous night.   31
Blind is his love and best befits the dark.
  Mercutio. If love be blind, love cannot hit the mark.
Now will he sit under a medlar tree   34
And wish his mistress were that kind of fruit
As maids call medlars when they laugh alone.
O, Romeo, that she were, O that she were
An open et cetera, thou a pop'rin pear!   38
Romeo, good night. I'll to my truckle-bed;   39
This field-bed is too cold for me to sleep.
Come shall we go?
  Benvolio.   Go then, for 'tis is vain
To seek him here that means not to be found.
                              [*Exit with others.*

Scene two.

(THE SAME. CAPULET'S ORCHARD)

Romeo. [*coming forward*] He jests at scars that
    never felt a wound.   1

Enter JULIET *above at a window.*

But soft! What light through yonder window breaks?
It is the East, and Juliet is the sun!
Arise, fair sun, and kill the envious moon,
Who is already sick and pale with grief
That thou her maid art far more fair than she.
Be not her maid, since she is envious.   7
Her vestal livery is but sick and green,   8
And none but fools do wear it. Cast it off.
It is my lady; O, it is my love!
O that she knew she were!
She speaks, yet she says nothing. What of that?
Her eye discourses; I will answer it.   13
I am too bold; 'tis not to me she speaks.
Two of the fairest stars in all the heaven,
Having some business, do entreat her eyes
To twinkle in their spheres till they return.
What if her eyes were there, they in her head?   18
The brightness of her cheek would shame those stars
As daylight doth a lamp; her eyes in heaven
Would through the airy region stream so bright
That birds would sing and think it were not night.
See how she leans her cheek upon her hand!
O that I were a glove upon that hand,
That I might touch that cheek!
  Juliet.   Ay me!
  Romeo.   She speaks.
O, speak again, bright angel! for thou art   26
As glorious to this night, being o'er my head,
As is a winged messenger of heaven
Unto the white-upturned wond'ring eyes   29

31. "humorous": damp (climate and physiology).

34. "medlar": a fruit like a small brown apple. The name lent itself to puns, of course.

38. "An open et cetera": a nice phrase for an unpleasant one.

39. "truckle-bed": small bed on wheels (cf. "truck") which (for a servant) was pushed under a larger bed (the master's). Mercutio means that even a truckle-bed would be better than "this field-bed."

1. "He . . . wound": Romeo is no doubt thinking of the scars made by Cupid's arrows, which Mercutio has never felt. This line is obviously a couplet with the previous one, before the change to the scene (not a change in place, however) which Romeo and Juliet have to themselves. The scene division is obviously wrong.

7. "Be not her maid": in other words, love and marry me.

8. "sick and green": Shakespeare is probably thinking of the "green-sickness," an anaemic disease causing a lingering death in young women (see III, v.156).
"vestal livery": virgin uniform.

13. "discourses": the language of love.

18. "they in": the stars in.

26. "thou": Romeo and Juliet address one another so ("thou" and "thee") as close friends. Bear in mind, however, that the address is imaginary to begin with—they do not actually speak to one another.

29. "white-upturned": the whites of the eyes turned upwards.

ROMEO AND JULIET

ACT II SCENE II

At this, Romeo emerges declaring that he will be "new baptized;" henceforth he "never will be Romeo."

Juliet is startled, recognizes Romeo, realizes she has revealed her secret to him, and fears for his safety if he is caught by her father's guards: "I would not for the world they saw thee here." She is both horrified at her betrayal of her modesty in the soliloquy that has suddenly transformed itself into a dialogue between lovers, and scared that her dear boy will come to harm on what is, after all, for him, enemy territory. She is relieved that the darkness hides her maidenly blushes, and says she would withdraw all she has said, and speak only formally. She asks Romeo to tell her if he loves her, but forbids him to swear by anything since Jove laughs at the perjuries of lovers. She is charming and natural in her embarrassment, and talks spontaneously and copiously to 'cover up'—she is desperately anxious not to be taken for a girl who loves lightly. Romeo swears his love for her is the real thing—and she confesses her joy in him; but their

Of mortals that fall back to gaze on him
When he bestrides the lazy-pacing clouds
And sails upon the bosom of the air.
    Juliet. O Romeo, Romeo! wherefore art thou Romeo?
Deny thy father and refuse thy name;
Or, if thou wilt not, be but sworn my love,
And I'll no longer be a Capulet.
    Romeo. [*aside*] Shall I hear more, or shall I speak at this?   37
    Juliet. 'Tis but thy name that is my enemy.
Thou art thyself, though not a Montague.
What's Montague? It is nor hand, nor foot,
Nor arm, nor face, nor any other part
Belonging to a man. O, be some other name!
What's in a name? That which we call a rose
By any other name would smell as sweet.
So Romeo would, were he not Romeo called,
Retain that dear perfection which he owes   46
Without that title. Romeo, doff thy name;   47
And for thy name, which is no part of thee,   48
Take all myself.
    Romeo.   I take thee at thy word.
Call me but love, and I'll be new baptized;   50
Henceforth I never will be Romeo.
    Juliet. What man art thou that, thus bescreened in night,
So stumblest on my counsel?   53
    Romeo.   By a name
I know not how to tell thee who I am.
My name, dear saint, is hateful to myself,
Because it is an enemy to thee.
Had I it written, I would tear the word.
    Juliet. My ears have yet not drunk a hundred words
Of thy tongue's uttering, yet I know the sound.
Art thou not Romeo, and a Montague?
    Romeo. Neither, fair maid, if either thee dislike.
    Juliet. How camest thou hither, tell me, and wherefore?
The orchard walls are high and hard to climb,
And the place death, considering who thou art,
If any of my kinsmen find thee here.
    Romeo. With love's light wings did I o'erperch   66
    these walls;
For stony limits cannot hold love out,   67
And what love can do, that dares love attempt.
Therefore thy kinsmen are no stop to me.
    Juliet. If they do see thee, they will murder thee.
    Romeo. Alack, there lies more peril in thine eye
Than twenty of their swords! Look thou but sweet,
And I am proof against their enmity.
    Juliet. I would not for the world they saw thee here.
    Romeo. I have night's cloak to hide me from their eyes;
And but thou love me, let them find me here.   76
My life were better ended by their hate
Than death prorogued, wanting of thy love.   78
    Juliet. By whose direction found'st thou out this place?
    Romeo. By love, that first did prompt me to inquire.

37. "this": this point, before she goes any farther.

46. "owes": possesses.

47. "doff": relinquish.

48. "for": in exchange for.

50. "new baptized": freshly renamed.

53. "stumblest on my counsel": overhears by accident my secret thoughts.

66. "o'erperch": fly over, a metaphor from a bird hopping from perch to perch.

67. "stony limits": boundaries of stone.

76. "but": except.
"them": the Capulets (enemies to Romeo, who is a Montague).

78. "prorogued": adjourned (postponed).

ROMEO AND JULIET

ACT II SCENE II

nocturnal meeting has occurred too rashly, too unadvisedly, too suddenly. They exchange vows, but the Nurse calls, and she has to go in. He waits, and she returns briefly, then has to go inside for good. She has arranged to send a messenger tomorrow at 9:00 a.m. to Romeo to discover what will be the time and place of their marriage. She says:

"all my fortunes at thy foot I'll lay,

And follow thee my lord throughout the world."

Romeo's lines are lyrical and idyllic. His:

"How silver-sweet sound lovers' tongues by night,

Life softest music to attending ears!"

is pure poetry, in which the felicity of the sibilants, the complex alliteration and assonance, the perfect correspondence of phonetic structure, emotive content, and form are of the highest lyrical value—without detracting from, and actually enhancing the dramatic action of the scene.

He lent me counsel, and I lent him eyes.   81
I am no pilot; yet, wert thou as far
As that vast shore washed with the farthest sea,
I should adventure for such merchandise.   84
Juliet. Thou knowest the mask of night is on my face;
Else would a maiden blush bepaint my cheek
For that which thou hast heard me speak to-night.
Fain would I dwell on form—fain, fain deny   88
What I have spoke; but farewell compliment!   89
Dost thou love me? I know thou wilt say 'Ay';
And I will take thy word. Yet, if thou swear'st,
Thou mayst prove false. At lovers' perjuries,
They say Jove laughs. O gentle Romeo,   93
If thou dost love, pronounce it faithfully.
Or if thou thinkest I am too quickly won,
I'll frown, and be perverse, and say thee nay,
So thou wilt woo; but else, not for the world.   97
In truth, fair Montague, I am too fond,   98
And therefore thou mayst think my 'haviour light: 99
But trust me, gentleman, I'll prove more true
Than those that have more cunning to be strange.   101
I should have been more strange, I must confess,
But that thou overheard'st, ere I was ware,
My true-love passion. Therefore pardon me,
And not impute this yielding to light love,
Which the dark night hath so discovered.
Romeo. Lady, by yonder blessed moon I vow,
That tips with silver all these fruit-tree tops—
Juliet. O, swear not by the moon, th' inconstant moon,   109
That monthly changes in her circled orb,   110
Lest that thy love prove likewise variable.
Romeo. What shall I swear by?
Juliet.   Do not swear at all;
Or if thou wilt, swear by thy gracious self,
Which is the god of my idolatry,   114
And I'll believe thee.
Romeo.   If my heart's dear love—
Juliet. Well, do not swear. Although I joy in thee,
I have no joy of this contract to-night.
It is too rash, too unadvised, too sudden;
Too like the lightning, which doth cease to be
Ere one can say 'It lightens.' Sweet, good night!
This bud of love, by summer's ripening breath,
May prove a beauteous flow'r when next we meet.
Good night, good night! As sweet repose and rest
Come to thy heart as that within my breast!
Romeo. O, wilt thou leave me so unsatisfied?
Juliet. What satisfaction canst thou have to-night?
Romeo. Th' exchange of thy love's faithful vow for mine.
Juliet. I gave thee mine before thou didst request it;
And yet I would it were to give again.   129
Romeo. Wouldst thou withdraw it? For what purpose, love?
Juliet. But to be frank and give it thee again.   131
And yet I wish but for the thing I have.   132
My bounty is as boundless as the sea,
My love as deep; the more I give to thee,

81. "I lent him eyes": Cupid is blind.

84. "merchandise": Juliet (note the sustained mercantile metaphor). "adventure for": speculate in—the regular word for overseas trading in Shakespeare's day.

88. "fain": gladly, willingly. "dwell on form": do the proper thing (in the formal, conventional way).

89. "farewell compliment!": goodby, polite conventions!

93. "Jove": King of the Roman gods.

97. "else": otherwise, i.e., I will not do this ("frown and be perverse and say thee nay") unless you think that "I am too quickly won."

98. "fond": foolish.

99. "'haviour": behavior (shortened because of the metrical necessity).

101. "strange": reserved, off-putting..

109. "inconstant": changeable or unfaithful.

110. "changes in her circled orb": referring to the moon's changes within the full circle; or, possibly, to the changes of the moon as it goes through its path in the heavens.

114. "Which . . . idolatry": which I worship (as if you were an idol).

129. "I would . . . again": so that I might have the pleasure all over again.

131. "frank": generous, bountiful.

132. "the thing I have": my love.

The more I have, for both are infinite.
I hear some noise within. Dear love, adieu!

[*Nurse* calls within.

Anon, good nurse! Sweet Montague, be true.
Stay but a little, I will come again.   [*Exit.*
  Romeo. O blessed, blessed night! I am afeard,
Being in night, all this is but a dream,
Too flattering-sweet to be substantial.   141

           Enter JULIET *above.*

  Juliet. Three words, dear Romeo, and good night
      indeed.
If that thy bent of love be honorable,
Thy purpose marriage, send me word to-morrow,
By one that I'll procure to come to thee,   145
Where and what time thou wilt perform the rite;
And all my fortunes at thy foot I'll lay
And follow thee my lord throughout the world.
  Nurse. [*within*] Madam!
  Juliet. I come, anon.—But if thou meanest not well, 150
I do beseech thee—
  Nurse. [*within*] Madam!
  Juliet.   By and by I come.—   152
To cease thy suit and leave me to my grief.
To-morrow will I send.
  Romeo.   So thrive my soul—
  Juliet. A thousand times good night!   [*Exit.*
  Romeo. A thousand times the worse, to want thy 156
    light!
Love goes toward love as schoolboys from their
    books;
But love from love, toward school with heavy looks.

        Enter JULIET, *above, again.*

  Juliet. Hist! Romeo, hist! O for a falc'ner's voice 159
To lure this tassel-gentle back again!   160
Bondage is hoarse and may not speak aloud,   161
Else would I tear the cave where Echo lies   162
And make her airy tongue more hoarse than mine 163
With repetition of 'My Romeo!'
  Romeo. It is my soul that calls upon my name.
How silver-sweet sound lovers' tongues by night, 166
Like softest music to attending ears!
  Juliet. Romeo!
  Romeo.   My sweet?
  Juliet.   At what o'clock to-morrow
Shall I send to thee?
  Romeo.   By the hour of nine.
  Juliet. I will not fail. 'Tis twenty years till then.
I have forgot why I did call thee back.
  Romeo. Let me stand here till thou remember it.
  Juliet. I shall forget, to have thee still stand there,
Rememb'ring how I love thy company.
  Romeo. And I'll still stay, to have thee still forget,
Forgetting any other home but this.
  Juliet. 'Tis almost morning. I would have thee gone—
And yet no farther than a wanton's bird,   178
That lets it hop a little from her hand,
Like a poor prisoner in his twisted gyves,   180
And with a silken thread plucks it back again,
So loving-jealous of his liberty.   182
  Romeo. I would I were thy bird.

Romeo's character has developed from the superficial yearning of adolescence to the commanding action, and authentic suffering of a person who knows the whole spectrum of manly feeling, despite his youthfulness.

141. "substantial": real.

145. "procure": cause, arrange.

150. "anon": in a short time (NOT immediately).

152. "By and by": at once (NOT in a short time).

156. "worse": worse night.
"to want thy light": being deprived of the light (cast by Juliet's presence).

159. "hist!": silence! or listen!
"falc'ner's voice": special tone employed to attract falcon back to the owner's wrist.

160. "tassel-gentle": male falcon of the peregrine variety.

161. "Bondage is hoarse": my bondage in (a secret) love makes me speak in a whisper.

162. "Echo": a mountain-nymph in Roman mythology (hence "the cave").

163. "airy tongue": the words Echo utters are so insubstantial that her tongue seems made merely of air.

166. "silver-sweet": as sweet as silver bells.

178. "wanton's bird": pet bird of an irresponsible girl, who (as is shown by what follows) teases her pets.

180. "gyves": chains (used to shackle prisoners).

182. "So loving-jealous of his liberty": so fond of the bird that she is jealous of its regaining its liberty.

ROMEO AND JULIET

ACT II SCENE II

Dramatically, this scene accomplishes the following purposes:

1. It presents to the audience the betrothal of Juliet and Romeo.

2. It illuminates their meeting with a spectacularly romantic feeling which is augmented by the picturesque setting (moonlight, danger, eavesdropping, exchange of vows, cheek, glove, window, garden, balcony, etc.).

3. The reference to the messenger prepares us for Friar Laurence.

ACT II SCENE III

It is now early Monday morning, the second day of the play's action. Romeo arrives at the cell of his confessor, Friar Laurence. The good Friar is already bustling with activity; he is about to search for medicinal herbs. This friar is to play a vital role as an herbalist, in the events about to be unfolded.

Friar Laurence, as revealed by his soliloquy, is kind and sympathetic, sensitive to nature and to beauty, and intent on healing by the judicious use of herbs, about which he speaks with knowledge. He has a philosophic turn, and remarks of one plant that, though it has a pleasant smell that "cheers each part," "being tasted," it "slays all senses with the heart." He concludes that just as good and evil coexist in herbs, so they do in men:

"And where the worser is predominant,

Full soon the canker death eats up that plant."

Juliet.   Sweet, so would I.
Yet I should kill thee with much cherishing.
Good night, good night! Parting is such sweet sorrow
That I shall say good night till it be morrow.   [*Exit.*
Romeo. Sleep dwell upon thine eyes, peace in thy breast!
Would I were sleep and peace, so sweet to rest!
Hence will I to my ghostly father's cell,   189
His help to crave and my dear hap to tell.   [*Exit.* 190

Scene three.

(THE SAME. FRIAR LAURENCE'S CELL)

Enter FRIAR LAURENCE *alone, with a basket.*

Friar. The grey-eyed morn smiles on the frowning night,
Check'ring the Eastern clouds with streaks of light;
And flecked darkness like a drunkard reels
From forth day's path and Titan's fiery wheels.   4
Now, ere the sun advance his burning eye
The day to cheer and night's dank dew to dry,
I must up-fill this osier cage of ours   7
With baleful weeds and precious-juiced flowers.   8
The earth that's nature's mother is her tomb.   9
What is her burying grave, that is her womb;
And from her womb children of divers kind
We sucking on her natural bosom find,
Many for many virtues excellent,
None but for some, and yet all different.   14
O, mickle is the powerful grace that lies   15
In plants, herbs, stones, and their true qualities;
For naught so vile that on the earth doth live
But to the earth some special good doth give;
Nor aught so good but, strained from that fair use,   19
Revolts from true birth, stumbling on abuse.
Virtue itself turns vice, being misapplied,
And vice sometimes 's by action dignified.   22

Enter ROMEO.

Within the infant rind of this weak flower   23
Poison hath residence, and medicine power;
For this, being smelt, with that part cheers each part;   25
Being tasted, slays all senses with the heart.   26
Two such opposed kings encamp them still
In man as well as herbs—grace and rude will;   28
And where the worser is predominant,
Full soon the canker death eats up that plant.   30
Romeo. Good morrow, father.
Friar.   Benedicite!   31
What early tongue so sweet saluteth me?
Young son, it argues a distempered head   33
So soon to bid good morrow to thy bed.
Care keeps his watch in every old man's eye,   35
And where care lodges, sleep will never lie;
But where unbruised youth with unstuffed brain   37
Doth couch his limbs, there golden sleep doth reign.   38
Therefore thy earliness doth me assure

---

189. "ghostly": pertaining to the Holy Ghost, spiritual father—priest who hears her confession and gives absolution.

190. "dear hap": good luck, good fortune.

4. "From forth": out of the way of. "Titan's": chariot belonging to the flaming god of the sun.

7. "osier cage": willow basket. "ours": the monastery to which he belonged.

8. "baleful": harmful, poisonous. "previous-juiced": containing wonderful properties in their juices.

9. "The earth . . . tomb": all life springs from the earth and when dead goes back to it. The next line contains the same thought, with the two parts in the reverse order.

14. "but for some": there are none which are not useful for something.

15. "mickle": great (Refer to the Scots proverb "mony a muckle maks a mickle.")

19. "strained": twisted away. "that fair use": the use for which it was intended.

22. "by action dignified": by the way it is used (presumably in a good cause) becomes dignified.

23. "infant rind": seedling stalk.

25. "that part": its scent.

26. "with the heart": by stopping ("slaying") the heart.

28. "grace and rude will": good and ill.

30. "canker": canker-worm.

31. "Benedicite!": an ecclesiastical greeting—"Bless (you)" or "Blessed be (God)!"

33. "argues": proves. "distempered": disturbed, upset, uneasy.

35. "his watch": awake.

37. "unbruised": unspoiled. "unstuffed": by care (anxiety).

38. "golden": priceless, invaluable.

ROMEO AND JULIET

ACT II SCENE III

Romeo enters, and the friar blesses him ("Benedicite"). Then, recognizing Romeo, he fears his earliness indicates a night of pleasure with Rosaline and is relieved to hear that Romeo has forgotten her. Romeo then tells of his love for Juliet, and requests the holy friar to perform their private wedding ceremony that very day. The friar belives Romeo is a turncoat in love, and charges him with insincerity. However, he consents to unite them later the same day because he hopes that this union will lead to an alliance between the two rival families.

This scene fulfils the following dramatic purposes:

1. Friar Laurence is introduced as an accomplished herbalist.

2. The arrangements for the immediate solemnization of Romeo's marriage to Juliet are completed.

3. It prepares us for the potion later given to Juliet by the friar.

4. The calm, philosophic speech of the friar gives peace and order to this scene, which is thereby distinguished from the turbulence and passion of the others in this play.

Thou art uproused with some distemp'rature; 40
Or if not so, then here I hit it right—
Our Romeo hath not been in bed to-night.
   Romeo. That last is true—the sweeter rest was mine.
   Friar. God pardon sin! Wast thou with Rosaline?
   Romeo. With Rosaline, my ghostly father? No.
I have forgot that name and that name's woe. 46
   Friar. That's my good son! But where hast thou
      been then?
   Romeo. I'll tell thee ere thou ask it me again.
I have been feasting with mine enemy, 49
Where on a sudden one hath wounded me 50
That's by me wounded. Both our remedies
Within thy help and holy physic lies.
I bear no hatred, blessed man, for lo,
My intercession likewise steads my foe. 54
   Friar. Be plain, good son, and homely in thy drift.
Riddling confession finds but riddling shrift. 56
   Romeo. Then plainly know my heart's dear love is
      set
On the fair daughter of rich Capulet;
As mine on hers, so hers is set on mine,
And all combined, save what thou must combine 60
By holy marriage. When, and where, and how
We met, we wooed, and made exchange of vow,
I'll tell thee as we pass; but this I pray,
That thou consent to marry us to-day.
   Friar. Holy Saint Francis! What a change is here!
Is Rosaline, that thou didst love so dear,
So soon forsaken? Young men's love then lies
Not truly in their hearts, but in their eyes.
Jesu Maria! What a deal of brine 69
Hath washed thy sallow cheeks for Rosaline!
How much salt water thrown away in waste
To season love, that of it doth not taste! 72
The sun not yet thy sighs from heaven clears, 73
Thy old groans ring yet in mine ancient ears.
Lo, here upon thy cheek the stain doth sit
Of an old tear that is not washed off yet.
If e'er thou wast thyself, and these woes thine, 77
Thou and these woes were all for Rosaline.
And art thou changed? Pronounce this sentence
      then:
Women may fall when there's no strength in men. 80
   Romeo. Thou chid'st me oft for loving Rosaline. 81
   Friar. For doting, not for loving, pupil mine. 82
   Romeo. And bad'st me bury love.
   Friar.   Not in a grave
To lay one in, another out to have. 84
   Romeo. I pray thee chide not. She whom I love now
Doth grace for grace and love for love allow. 86
The other did not so.
   Friar.   O, she knew well
Thy love did read by rote, that could not spell. 88
But come, young waverer, come go with me.
In one respect I'll thy assistant be; 90
For this alliance may so happy prove
To turn your households' rancor to pure love. 92
   Romeo. O, let us hence! I stand on sudden haste.
   Friar. Wisely and slow. They stumble that run fast.
                      [*Exeunt.*

40. "distemp'rature": disturbance of of mind (probably accompanied by physical disturbance).

46. "that name's woe": the woe Rosaline brought me (by rejecting my suit).

49. "mine enemy": the Capulets.

50. "one": refers to Juliet. "wounded": by love.

54. "steads": benefits.

56. "Riddling": puzzling, doubtful. "shrift": forgiveness and pardon.

60. "combined": agreed. "combine": unite. The word is used in two senses in the line.

69. "Maria": Son of Mary. "brine": salt water (tears).

72. "season": preserve (by salt water, the same word as in "seasoning." Salting and drying were the two chief methods of preserving in Shakespeare's days. "it": true love.

73. "sighs": Romeo's sighs for Rosaline are thought of as clouds rising into the air. Cf. what Romeo says in I.i, "Love is a smoke raised with the fume of sighs."

77. "thyself": true to thyself. "thine": genuine.

80. "Women may": no wonder women do. "fall": fall from grace (be unfaithful).

81. "chid'st": rebuked.

82. "doting": unreasoning infatuation.

84. "to lay one . . . have": as if you are on with the new love almost before you are off with the old.

86. "grace for grace": favor in return for favor.

88. "did read . . . spell": had learnt it by heart and could not read, i.e., you repeated the words of love without understanding what love meant.

90. "In one respect": on account of one thing.

92. "households' rancor": bitterness between the two families.

ACT II SCENE IV

At 9:00 a.m. Juliet's messenger, the Nurse, is searching for Romeo; so are Mercutio and Benvolio. Benvolio has discovered that Romeo did not spend last night at home, and that a letter, presumably containing a challenge, from Tybalt, "prince of cats," is waiting for Romeo. Mercutio fears that, in his lovelorn state, Romeo will be no match for Tybalt. Mercutio is very interested in dueling, and introduces some recent technical terms taken from Italian and French dueling practices (passado, punto reverso, the hay). He is expatiating on these execrable new foreign terms — "these strange flies" — when Romeo enters.

Mercutio expects Romeo to be in low spirits, and puns on the first syllable of the name: Ro(e) —nothing left—O! Romeo ignores this and the sarcastic list of women that follows, and jests merrily with the Nurse, puffing with self-importance, finds him. Mercutio ridicules her, and she is indignant. Romeo then reveals his identity, and she says she has a private message for him, so the others leave—still mocking her.

The Nurse tries to sound out Romeo's intentions, but in her quivering indignation, misunderstands Romeo's use of the verb "protest," takes if for an assurance of integrity, and says she will tell Juliet, who will be a "joyfull woman" on hearing this news. "What wilt thou tell her, nurse? thou dost not mark me."—replies Romeo, then gets down to details.

Scene four.

(THE SAME. A STREET)

Enter BENVOLIO *and* MERCUTIO.

Mercutio. Where the devil should this Romeo be?
Came he not home to-night? 2

Benvolio. Not to his father's. I spoke with his man.

Mercutio. Why, that same pale hard-hearted wench, that Rosaline,
Torments him so that he will sure run mad.

Benvolio. Tybalt, the kinsman to old Capulet,
Hath sent a letter to his father's house.

Mercutio. A challenge, on my life.

Benvolio. Romeo will answer it.

Mercutio. Any man that can write may answer a letter.

Benvolio. Nay, he will answer the letter's master, how he dares, being dared.

Mercutio. Alas, poor Romeo, he is already dead! stabbed with a white wench's black eye; run through the ear with a love song; the very pin of his heart 15
cleft with the blind bow-boy's butt-shaft; and is he a 16
man to encounter Tybalt? 17

Benvolio. Why, what is Tybalt?

Mercutio. More than Prince of Cats, I can tell you. 19
O, he's the courageous captain of compliments. He fights as you sing pricksong—keeps time, distance, 21
and proportion; he rests his minim rests, one, two, 22
and the third in your bosom! the very butcher of a 23
silk button, a duellist, a duellist! a gentleman of the 24
very first house, of the first and second cause. Ah, 25
the immortal passado! the punto reverso! the hay!

Benvolio. The what?

Mercutio. The pox of such antic, lisping, affecting fantasticoes—these new tuners of accent! 'By Jesu, 29
a very good blade! a very tall man! a very good 30
whore!' Why, is not this a lamentable thing, grandsir, 31
that we should be thus afflicted with these strange flies, these fashion-mongers, these pardon-me's, who 33
stand so much on the new form that they cannot sit at ease on the old bench? O, their bones, their bones!

Enter ROMEO.

Benvolio. Here comes Romeo! here comes Romeo!

Mercutio. Without his roe, like a dried herring. O 37
flesh, flesh, how art thou fishified! Now is he for the numbers that Petrarch flowed in. Laura, to his lady, 39
was a kitchen wench (marry, she had a better love to berhyme her), Dido a dowdy, Cleopatra a gypsy, 41
Helen and Hero hildings and harlots, Thisbe a grey 42
eye or so, but not to the purpose. Signior Romeo, bon jour! There's a French salutation to your French slop. 44
You gave us the counterfeit fairly last night.

Romeo. Good morrow to you both. What counterfeit did I give you?

Mercutio. The slip, sir, the slip. Can you not conceive? 48

2. "to-night": last night.

15. "pin": center-pin. In archery competitions the white target was fastened to a post by a wooden pin: it was thus a sign of extremely good marksmanship to hit the pin in the very center.

16. "butt-shaft": arrow used in archery practice at the butts (mounds of earth behind the targets, as used in rifle practice today).

17. "man": fit and proper person.

19. "Prince of Cats": in the old story of Reynard the Fox, the cat is called "Tibert" or "Tybert," a variant of the name Tybalt (Theobald), and it was a name often given to cats (cf. the modern "Tibby").

21. "pricksong": music noted down exactly.

22. "minim": short note in music.

23-24. "butcher of a silk button": the mark of a good duellist, the sort of thing young men used to boast about in those days.

24-25. "a gentleman . . . cause": expert at duelling.

25. "house": rank (of duellists).

29. "fantasticoes": absurd, irrational persons.
"new tuners of accents": speakers in the latest fashion, who affect all the new idioms and mannerisms of speech.

30. "blade": fighter (metonymy).
"tall": spirited, bold.

31. "grandsir": said humorously to Benvolio, who is not one of "these new tuners of accents."

33. "flies": implying that they are always buzzing about.

37. "roe": punning on his name, and perhaps also on "roe," a female deer, i.e., without his lady-love.

39. "numbers": (lines of) poetry.

41. "Dido": the first of a list of beautiful lovers famous in classical mythology (and Elizabethan literature derived from it). Dido, Queen of Carthage, killed herself when Æneas deserted her.

42. "Hero": whose lover, Leander, swam nightly across Hellespont to see her. "hildings": mean, low women. "Thisbe": lover of Pyramus. In the face of parental opposition their love ended in a way not unlike that of Romeo and Juliet.

44. "slop": baggy (sloppy) trousers.

48. "slip": a term for counterfeit coin. Here it is used with a double meaning.

He sends a message asking Juliet to meet him at Friar Laurence's cell that afternoon to be confessed, absolved, and married. He bribes the Nurse and arranges for her to meet one of his own men who will bring a rope ladder so that Romeo will be able to climb to Juliet's bedroom "in the secret night." The nurse falls in with this plan, and begins to gossip about Juliet and Paris, and about Romeo and Rosemary, savoring the implications like a procuress—with whose character, indeed, she has much in common.

Romeo. Pardon, good Mercutio. My business was great, and in such a case as mine a man may strain courtesy.

Mercutio. That's as much as to say, such a case as yours constrains a man to bow in the hams. 53

Romeo. Meaning, to curtsy.

Mercutio. Thou hast most kindly hit it. 55

Romeo. A most courteous exposition.

Mercutio. Nay, I am the very pink of courtesy.

Romeo. Pink for flower. 58

Mercutio. Right.

Romeo. Why, then is my pump well-flowered. 60

Mercutio. Sure wit, follow me this jest now till thou hast worn out thy pump, that, when the single sole of 62 it is worn, the jest may remain, after the wearing, solely singular. 64

Romeo. O single-soled jest, solely singular for the singleness!

Mercutio. Come between us, good Benvolio! My 66 wits faint.

Romeo. Swits and spurs, swits and spurs! or I'll cry a match. 67

Mercutio. Nay, if our wits run the wild-goose chase, 68 I am done; for thou hast more of the wild goose in one of thy wits than, I am sure, I have in my whole five. Was I with you there for the goose? 71

Romeo. Thou wast never with me for anything when thou wast not there for the goose. 73

Mercutio. I will bite thee by the ear for that jest. 74

Romeo. Nay, good goose, bite not!

Mercutio. Thy wit is a very bitter sweeting; it is a 76 most sharp sauce. 77

Romeo. And is it not, then, well served in to a sweet goose?

Mercutio. O, here's a wit of cheveril, that stretches 79 from an inch narrow to an ell broad!

Romeo. I stretch it out for that word 'broad,' which 81 added to the goose, proves thee far and wide a broad goose.

Mercutio. Why, is not this better now than groaning for love? Now art thou sociable, now art thou Romeo; now art thou what thou art, by art as well as by nature. For this drivelling love is like a great natural that runs lolling up and down to hide his bauble in a 87 hole.

Benvolio. Stop there, stop there!

Mercutio. Thou desirest me to stop in my tale against the hair. 89

Benvolio. Thou wouldst else have made thy tale large. 91

Mercutio. O, thou art deceived! I would have made it short; for I was come to the whole depth of my tale, and meant indeed to occupy the argument no longer.

Romeo. Here's goodly gear! 95

Enter Nurse *and her Man* PETER.

Mercutio. A sail, a sail!

Benvolio. Two, two! a shirt and a smock. 97

Nurse. Peter!

Peter. Anon. 99

Nurse. My fan, Peter. 100

53. "hams": knees.

55. "kindly": suitably.
"it": my meaning.

58. "flower": referring to the phrase, "The Flower of courtesy."

60. "pump": court shoe (taking up "courtesy"). A "pinked" shoe was punched with holes in patterns. "flowered": decorated.

62. "single sole": a pump was made with a single sole, for lightness in dancing (not with a sole added to the shoe, which could be replaced when worn).

64. "solely singular": the bare (soles of the) feet.

66. "My wits faint": at Romeo's cleverness. (He is being sarcastic, of course).

67. "match": contest. By a metaphor from horse racing Romeo says, "Let's carry on with the contest—even although your wits faint—or I'll challenge you."

68. "the wild-goose chase": my following you. The term "wild-goose chase" was applied to a contest where two riders started together and as soon as one obtained the lead the other had to follow over the same ground, unless he could overtake him, when the position was reversed. The name is taken from the way a flock of geese flies in a line. The phrase has a rather different meaning now.

71. "Was I with you there": did you see my point?

73. "not there for the goose": not there to play the part of, to act as silly as, a goose. Romeo replies taking "with me" literally.

74. "bite thee by the ear": a term of endearment, not of assault.

76. "sweeting": a very sweet kind of apple. The word was used metaphorically as a term of endearment.

77. "sauce": referring to the apple sauce usually served with roast goose.

79. "cheveril": kid.

81. "it": my wit.

87. "bauble": short stick, or baton, of the clown.

89. "against the hair": or, as we say, "against the grain," a metaphor from brushing the hair of an animal the opposite way to which it lies. The pun on "tale" (tail) is obvious, of course.

91. "large": punning on the sense "vulgar," "broad."

95. "goodly gear": said in reference to the Nurse, who, as she comes, looks like a bundle of clothes.

97. "a shirt and a smock": a man and a woman.

99. "Anon!": coming presently.

100. "fan": fans were very large in those days and it was not uncommon for them to be carried by a servant.

ROMEO AND JULIET

ACT II SCENE IV

This scene fulfils the following dramatic purposes:

1. The arrangements for the marriage are complete.

2. The characters of Mercutio and the Nurse are developed in greater depth.

3. The humor in the scene lightens the play in view of the tragic events that await the unfolding.

4. The emphasis on dueling prepares us for an important duel (Mercutio's) later on.

Mercutio. Good Peter, to hide her face; for her fan's the fairer face.

Nurse. God ye good morrow, gentlemen.　103

Mercutio. God ye good-den, fair gentlewoman.　104

Nurse. Is it good-den?　105

Mercutio. 'Tis no less, I tell ye; for the bawdy hand of the dial is now upon the prick of noon.

Nurse. Out upon you! What a man are you!

Romeo. One, gentlewoman, that God hath made for himself to mar.

Nurse. By my troth, it is well said. 'For himself to mar,' quoth 'a? Gentlemen, can any of you tell me where I may find the young Romeo?　112

Romeo. I can tell you; but young Romeo will be older when you have found him than he was when you sought him. I am the youngest of that name, for fault of a worse.　114

Nurse. You say well.

Mercutio. Yea, is the worst well? Very well took, i' faith! wisely, wisely.

Nurse. If you be he, sir, I desire some confidence with you.　120

Benvolio. She will endite him to some supper.　121

Mercutio. A bawd, a bawd, a bawd! So ho!　122

Romeo. What hast thou found?

Mercutio. No hare, sir; unless a hare, sir, in a lenten pie, that is something stale and hoar ere it be spent.　124　125

He walks by them and sings.

> An old hare hoar,
> And an old hare hoar,
> Is very good meat in Lent;
> But a hare that is hoar
> Is too much for a score
> When it hoars ere it be spent.

Romeo, will you come to your father's? We'll to dinner thither.

Romeo. I will follow you.

Mercutio. Farewell, ancient lady. Farewell,
Sings. lady, lady, lady.　[*Exeunt* MERCUTIO, BENVOLIO.

Nurse. I pray you, sir, what saucy merchant was this that was so full of his ropery?　137　138

Romeo. A gentleman, nurse, that loves to hear himself talk and will speak more in a minute than he will stand to in a month.

Nurse. An 'a speak anything against me, I'll take him down, an 'a were lustier than he is, and twenty such Jacks; and if I cannot, I'll find those that shall. Scurvy knave! I am none of his flirt-gills; I am none of his skains-mates. And thou must stand by too, and suffer every knave to use me at his pleasure!　143　144　145

Peter. I saw no man use you at his pleasure. If I had, my weapon should quickly have been out, I warrant you. I dare draw as soon as another man, if I see occasion in a good quarrel, and the law on my side.

Nurse. Now, afore God, I am so vexed that every part about me quivers. Scurvy knave! Pray you, sir, a word; and, as I told you, my young lady bid me inquire you out. What she bid me say, I will keep to

103. "God ye": God give you.

104. "God ye good-den": God give you good evening.

105. "Is it good-den?" is it as late as that (after mid-day)?

112. "'a": he.

114. "will . . . sought him": Romeo thinks that she will be wordy.

120. "confidence": malapropism (she means 'conference').

121. "endite": malapropism (he means 'invite') Benvolio mimics the Nurse.

122. "bawd": go-between a man and a woman.

124. "hare": woman of loose character.

125. "lenten pie": a poor sort of a pie. "hoar": mouldy.

137. "merchant": fellow—in a disparaging sense. Still so used in Warwickshire.

138. "ropery": roguery.

143. "Jacks": knaves.

144. "flirt-gills": loose women. "Gill" was a familiar or contemptuous term for a girl (as "Jack" for a boy).

145. "skains-mates": loose women.

myself; but first let me tell ye, if ye should lead her into a fool's paradise, as they say, it were a very gross kind of behavior, as they say; for the gentlewoman is young; and therefore, if you should deal double with her, truly it were an ill thing to be offered to any gentlewoman, and very weak dealing. 160

Romeo. Nurse, commend me to thy lady and mis- 161
  tress. I protest unto thee—

Nurse. Good heart, and i' faith I will tell her as 163
much. Lord, Lord! she will be a joyful woman.

Romeo. What wilt thou tell her, nurse? Thou dost 165
not mark me.

Nurse. I will tell her, sir, that you do protest, which,
as I take it, is a gentlemanlike offer.

Romeo. Bid her devise
Some means to come to shrift this afternoon; 170
And there she shall at Friar Laurence' cell
Be shrived and married. Here is for thy pains. 172

Nurse. No, truly, sir; not a penny.

Romeo. Go to! I say you shall. 174

Nurse. This afternoon, sir? Well, she shall be there.

Romeo. And stay, good nurse, behind the abbey wall.
Within this hour my man shall be with thee
And bring thee cords made like a tackled stair, 178
Which to the high topgallant of my joy 179
Must be my convoy in the secret night.
Farewell. Be trusty, and I'll quit thy pains. 181
Farewell. Commend me to thy mistress.

Nurse. Now God in heaven bless thee! Hark you, sir.

Romeo. What say'st thou, my dear nurse?

Nurse. Is your man secret? Did you ne'er hear say,
Two may keep counsel, putting one away? 186

Romeo. I warrant thee my man's as true as steel.

Nurse. Well, sir, my mistress is the sweetest lady.
Lord, Lord! when 'twas a little prating thing—O, 189
there is a nobleman in town, one Paris, that would
fain lay knife aboard; but she, good soul, had a 191
lieve see a toad, a very toad, as see him. I anger her
sometimes, and tell her that Paris is the properer 193
man; but I'll warrant you, when I say so, she looks
as pale as any clout in the versal world. Doth not 194
rosemary and Romeo begin both with a letter? 195

Romeo. Ay, nurse; what of that? Both with an R.

Nurse. Ah, mocker! that's the dog's name. R is for 197
the—No; I know it begins with some other letter;
and she hath the prettiest sententious of it, of you 199
and rosemary, that it would do you good to hear it.

Romeo. Commend me to thy lady.

Nurse. Ay, a thousand times. [*Exit* ROMEO.] Peter!

Peter. Anon.

Nurse. [*Peter, take my fan, and go*] before, and 204
  apace.   [*Exit after* PETER.

160. "and very weak dealing": this anti-climax is typical of a "weak" intelligence and a wordy tongue—going on for the sake of it.

161. "commend me": corresponding to our "remember me" (lit. recommend me).

163. "Good heart": my good fellow.

165. "thou": notice that generally (but not invariably) Romeo addresses the Nurse as "thou" and that she addresses him as "you".

170. "shrift": confession (where she would receive shrift, or absolution).

172. "shrived": absolved from her sins and forgiven.

174. "Go to ": nonsense

178. "tackled stair": roped ladder.

179. "topgallant": highest sail on the mast; hence, summit.

181. "quit": requite, reward (thee for).

186. "Two may keep counsel . . .": TWO can keep a secret, but not THREE. "putting one away": If there is only one there.

189. "prating": empty foolish talking.

191. "lay knife aboard": possess her. "as lieve": as soon.

193. "properer": more handsome.

194. "clout": a piece of cloth. "versal": universal (whole).

195. "rosemary": the flower symbolical of remembrance, and hence used at weddings and (see IV. v. 78) at funerals.
"a letter": a common letter, "R".

197. "dog's name": dog's letter or sound, known as 'littera canina' because, when rolled, "r" sounds like a dog's growling.

199. "sententious": he means sentences. The nurse often uses words with the wrong sense (malapropisms).

204. "before": go before me. "apace": quickly.

ACT II SCENE V

Juliet is alone in Capulet's garden, waiting for the Nurse, who promised to return in half an hour. She is walking up and down, weighing thoughts of failure and success, and anxiously imagining reasons to explain the Nurse's delay. There is a dramatic pause at the end of line 15; soon afterwards the Nurse and Peter enter.

Scene five.

(THE SAME. CAPULET'S GARDEN)

Enter JULIET.

Juliet. The clock struck nine when I did send the
    nurse;
In half an hour she promised to return.
Perchance she cannot meet him. That's not so.
O, she is lame! Love's herald's should be thoughts,   4
Which ten times faster glide than the sun's beams
Driving back shadows over low'ring hills.   6
Therefore do nimble-pinioned doves draw Love,   7
And therefore hath the wind-swift Cupid wings.
Now is the sun upon the highmost hill
Of this day's journey, and from nine till twelve
Is three long hours; yet she is not come.
Had she affections and warm youthful blood,
She would be as swift in motion as a ball;
My words would bandy her to my sweet love,   14
And his to me.
But old folks, many feign as they were dead—
Unwieldly, slow, heavy and pale as lead.

Enter Nurse *and* PETER.

O God, she comes! O honey nurse, what news?   18
Hast thou met with him? Send thy man away.
    Nurse. Peter, stay at the gate.   [*Exit* PETER.
    Juliet. Now, good sweet nurse—O Lord, why look-
    est thou sad?
Though news be sad, yet tell them merrily;
If good, thou shamest the music of sweet news
By playing it to me with so sour a face.
    Nurse. I am aweary, give me leave awhile.
Fie, how my bones ache! What a jaunce have I had!   26
    Juliet. I would thou hadst my bones, and I thy news.
Nay, come, I pray thee speak. Good, good nurse,
    speak.
    Nurse. Jesu, what haste! Can you not stay awhile?
Do you not see that I am out of breath?
    Juliet. How art thou out of breath when thou hast
    breath
To say to me that thou art out of breath?
The excuse that thou dost make in this delay
Is longer than the tale thou dost excuse.   34
Is thy news good or bad? Answer to that.
Say either, and I'll stay the circumstance.   36
Let me be satisfied, is't good or bad?
    Nurse. Well, you have made a simple choice; you   38
know not how to choose a man. Romeo? No, not he.
Though his face be better than any man's, yet his leg
excels all men's; and for a hand and a foot, and a
body, though they be not to be talked on, yet they are
past compare. He is not the flower of courtesy, but,   42
I'll warrant him, as gentle as a lamb. Go thy ways,
wench; serve God. What, have you dined at home?   44
    Juliet. No, no. But all this did I know before.
What says he of our marriage? What of that?

4. "lame": figuratively speaking, of course.

6. "low'ring": dark and threatening.

7. "nimble-pinioned doves": nimble-winged doves.
"doves": the Chariot of Venus was drawn by doves, which were sacred to her.

14. "bandy": toss or hit (her).

18. "honey": sweet.

26. "jaunce": trudging about.

34. "excuse": excuse thyself from telling.

36. "circumstance": details.

38. "simple": stupid, foolish.

42. "compare": comparison.

44. "serve God": enough of that.

ACT II SCENE V

Juliet clamors for news, but the Nurse teases her by keeping her waiting while she complains of weariness, aching bones and breathlessness etc. Finally, when poor Juliet is out of all patience, Nurse tells her to be at the Friar's cell this afternoon to be married to her Romeo. She also reveals that she is to find a ladder with which Romeo will "climb a bird's nest soon when it is dark."

The dramatic purposes of this scene are as follows:

1. It provides suspense for both Juliet and the audience.

2. It reveals hitherto unsuspected aspects of the nurse and her young mistress.

3. It supplies comic relief to lighten the forthcoming blackness by contrast.

ACT II SCENE VI

Romeo, after having gone to Friar Laurence's cell to make his confession, is waiting for Juliet to do likewise. The scene opens with Romeo's echoing a pious "Amen" to the friar's hope that the heaven will smile upon the marriage, "That after hours with sorrow chide us not." Did the holy man have a premonition of the awful chiding he would be shortly visited with? Observe the careful art with which Shakespeare prepares us, step by step, for what is to come.

Juliet enters so lightly of foot that Friar Laurence says that her foot will never wear out "the ever-

---

Nurse. Lord, how my head aches! What a head have I!
It beats as it would fall in twenty pieces.
My back a t' other side—ah, my back, my back! 50
Beshrew your heart for sending me about 51
To catch my death with jauncing up and down!
 Juliet. I' faith, I am sorry that thou art not well.
Sweet, sweet, sweet nurse, tell me, what says my love?
 Nurse. Your love says, like an honest gentleman, and a courteous, and kind, and handsome, and, I warrant, a virtuous—Where is your mother?
 Juliet. Where is my mother? Why, she is within.
Where should she be? How oddly thou repliest!
'Your love says, like an honest gentleman,
"Where is your mother?"'
 Nurse.   O God's Lady dear! 62
Are you so hot? Marry come up, I trow. 63
Is this the poultice for my aching bones?
Henceforward do your messages yourself.
 Juliet. Here's such a coil! Come, what says Romeo? 65
 Nurse. Have you got leave to go to shrift to-day?
 Juliet. I have.
 Nurse. Then hie you hence to Friar Laurence' cell; 68
There stays a husband to make you a wife.
Now comes the wanton blood up in your cheeks:
They'll be in scarlet straight at any news. 71
Hie you to church; I must another way,
To fetch a ladder, by the which your love
Must climb a bird's nest soon when it is dark.
I am the drudge, and toil in your delight;
But you shall bear the burden soon at night.
Go; I'll to dinner; hie you to the cell.
 Juliet. Hie to high fortune! Honest nurse farwell.
                                        [*Exeunt.*

Scene six.

(THE SAME. FRIAR LAURENCE'S CELL)

Enter FRIAR LAURENCE *and* ROMEO.

Friar. So smile the heavens upon this holy act 1
That after-hours with sorrow chide us not! 2
 Romeo. Amen, amen! But come what sorrow can,
It cannot countervail the exchange of joy 4
That one short minute gives me in her sight.
Do thou but close our hands with holy words,
Then love-devouring death to what he dare—
It is enough I may but call her mine.
 Friar. These violent delights have violent ends
And in their triumph die, like fire and powder,
Which, as they kiss, consume. The sweetest honey
Is loathsome in his own deliciousness 12
And in the taste confounds the appetite.
Therefore love moderately: long love doth so; 14
Too swift arrives as tardy as too slow. 15

---

50. "a t' other": on the other.
51. "Beshrew": curse.

62. "God's Lady dear!": The Virgin Mary.

63. "hot": eager.
"come up, I trow": a colloquial expression of impatience, as we might say, "Come, come."

65. "coil": trouble, fuss.

68. "hie": hasten.

71. "be in scarlet": blush (because Juliet has a guilty conscience).

1. "smile": may heaven favor.
2. "after-hours": the future.
4. "countervail": outweigh.
"the exchange of joy": the joy for which it is taken in return.

12. "Is loathsome in his own deliciousness": it is so sweet that it soon becomes sickly.

14. "doth so": that is, is moderate.

15. "Too swift . . . slow": in words of our proverb, "more haste, less speed."

ROMEO AND JULIET

ACT II SCENE VI

lasing flint'' of life's care. This may me be yet another premonition of disaster. Romeo begs Juliet to:

"... sweeten with thy breath
This neighbor air, and let rich music's tongue
Unfold the imagined happiness..."

but she replies that her "true love is grown to such excess" she "cannot sum up sum of HALF" her wealth, let alone ALL of it.

They follow the friar into the chantry, there to be incorporated, two in one body.

The dramatic purpose achieved by the terminal scene of the second act are as follows:
1. To announce to the audience the marriage of the lovers.
2. To close the act with outward success overshadowed by omens of impending catastrophe.

Enter JULIET.

Here comes the lady. O, so light a foot
Will ne'er wear out the everlasting flint. 17
A lover may bestride the gossamer 18
That idles in the wanton summer air,
And yet not fall; so light is vanity. 20
Juliet. Good even to my ghostly confessor. 21
Friar. Romeo shall thank thee, daughter, for us both. 22
Juliet. As much to him, else is his thanks too much. 23
Romeo. Ah, Juliet, if the measure of thy joy
Be heaped like mine, and that thy skill be more
To blazon it, then sweeten with thy breath 26
This neighbor air, and let rich music's tongue 27
Unfold the imagined happiness that both 28
Receive in either by this dear encounter.
Juliet. Conceit, more rich in matter than in words, 30
Brags of his substance, not of ornament. 31
They are but beggars that can count their worth;
But my true love is grown to such excess
I cannot sum up sum of half my wealth.
Friar. Come, come with me, and we will make short work;
For, by your leaves, you shall not stay alone 36
Till Holy Church incorporate two in one. [*Exeunt.*

17. "wear out": outlast.

18. "gossamer": long single thread of a spider's web.

20. "vanity": emptiness.

21. "confessor": priest who listens to confessions.

22. "thank thee": return your greeting. The Friar says that he will leave Romeo to say good evening (or thank you), implying that Romeo is anxious to speak to her.

23. "As much": refers back to "good even"—as much as to say 'good evening.'

26. "blazon it": spread it abroad, broadcast it.

27. "neighbor": neighboring.
"rich music's tongue": Juliet's voice.

28. "imagined happiness": mental imaginative happiness.

30. "Conceit": thought, fancy, imagination.

31. "ornament": show. Juliet says that the real thing means more to her than any words can say.

36. "by your leaves": if you will obey my orders.

45

ROMEO AND JULIET

ACT III SCENE I

This scene contains the death of Tybalt and the banishment of Romeo from Verona—events that constitute the crisis, or turning point, of the dramatic action.

Benvolio, Mercutio, and their followers are cavorting together in Verona's public square; Benvolio advises going home in case they meet any of the Capulets there. He wishes to avoid a brawl, but Mercutio is spoiling for a fight, and accuses his friend of not really wanting peace, either. Tybalt and some other members of the rival house now enter, and address Mercutio. He wishes to learn Romeo's whereabouts, but Mercutio forestalls him by demanding action before words.

Despite Benvolio's imploring, they are about to fight there in the public place when Romeo appears; Tybalt leaves Mercutio standing, and turns towards Romeo, calling him "villain." Romeo, fresh from his marriage, does not wish to fight Juliet's cousin, but he denies he is a villain. Romeo says he loves all Capulets. Mercutio cannot stand this dishonorable submission and dares Tybalt to fight with him. The duel commences, and in the subsequent confusion Tybalt reaches under Romeo's arm and wounds Mercutio.

ACT THREE, scene one.

(VERONA. A PUBLIC PLACE)

Enter MERCUTIO, BENVOLIO, *and* Men.

Benvolio. I pray thee, good Mercutio, let's retire. 1
The day is hot, the Capulets abroad, 2
And, if we meet, we shall not 'scape a brawl,
For now, these hot days, is the mad blood stirring. 4
Mercutio. Thou are like one of these fellows that,
when he enters the confines of a tavern, claps me his 6
sword upon the table and says 'God send me no
need of thee!' and by the operation of the second 8
cup draws him on the drawer, when indeed there is 9
no need.
Benvolio. Am I like such a fellow?
Mercutio. Come, come, thou art as hot a Jack in 11
thy mood as any in Italy; and as soon moved to be 12
moody, and as soon moody to be moved.
Benvolio. And what to? 14
Mercutio. Nay, and there were two such, we should 15
have none shortly, for one would kill the other. Thou!
why, thou wilt quarrel with a man that hath a hair
more or a hair less in his beard than thou hast. Thou
wilt quarrel with a man for cracking nuts, having no
other reason but because thou hast hazel eyes. What 20
eye but such an eye would spy out such a quarrel?
Thy head is as full of quarrels as an egg is full of
meat; and yet thy head hath been beaten as addle 23
as an egg for quarrelling. Thou hast quarrelled with
a man for coughing in the street, because he hath
wakened thy dog that hath lain asleep in the sun.
Didst thou not fall out with a tailor for wearing his 26
new doublet before Easter? with another for tying 27
his new shoes with old riband? And yet thou wilt
tutor me from quarrelling! 29
Benvolio. An I were so apt to quarrel as thou art,
any man should buy the fee simple of my life for an 31
hour and a quarter. 32
Mercutio. The fee simple? O simple! 33

Enter TYBALT *and others.*

Benvolio. By my head, here come the Capulets.
Mercuito. By my heel, I care not.
Tybalt. Follow me close, for I will speak to them.
Gentlemen, good-den. A word with one of you. 37
Mercuito. And but one word with one of us?
Couple it with something; make it a word and a blow.
Tybalt. You shall find me apt enough to that, sir, an
you will give me occasion. 41
Mercutio. Could you not take some occasion without giving? 43
Tybalt. Mercutio, thou consortest with Romeo. 44
Mercutio. Consort? What, dost thou make us 45
minstrels?
An thou make minstrels of us, look to hear nothing
but discords. Here's my fiddlestick; here's that 47
shall make you dance. Zounds, consort! 48
Benvolio. We talk here in the public haunt of men.

---

1. "retire": go away from the crowds.

2. "abroad": out and about.

4. "blood": temper, fury.

6. "me": let me tell you—the dative form was idiomatic in Shakespeare's speech.

8. "by the operation of the second cup": by the time the second cup of liquor has worked upon him.

9. "drawer": waiter or barman.

11. "Jack": fellow.

12. "moved": provoked or incited. "moody": bad tempered.

14. "what to?": provoked to what?

15. "two": Mercutio Benvolio's "to" as "two."

20. "hazel": the color of hazel NUTS.

23. "meat": food, not necessarily flesh. CF. the phrase "meat and drink." "addle": mixed up and, perhaps, rotten.

26. "fall out with": quarrel with a friend.

27. "doublet": close-fitting body garment, with or without sleeves, worn by men from the 14th to the 18th century.

29. "tutor me from quarrelling": teach me how to avoid getting into quarrels.

31. "fee simple": complete legal rights over (by purchase).

31-32. "for an hour and a quarter": implying that by the end of that time he would be dead (dramatic irony).

33. "simple": foolish!

37. "good-den": good evening (means good afternoon).

41. "occasion": excuse.

43. "giving": being given one.

44. "consortest": keep company with, or keep in tune with.

45. "Consort!": the regular word for harmony among players, or for an actual group of fiddlers. Out for a quarrel, Mercutio gives the word its worst sense—wandering fiddler.

45. "make us minstrels": call us (set us down as) vagabond fiddlers.

47. "fiddlestick": his sword.

48. "Zounds": a contraction of the oath, "By God's wounds" (i.e., on the Cross).

Either withdraw unto some private place,
Or reason coldly of your grievances, 51
Or else depart. Here all eyes gaze on us.
 Mercutio. Men's eyes were made to look, and let them gaze.
I will not budge for no man's pleasure, I.

 Enter ROMEO.

 Tybalt. Well, peace be with you, sir. Here comes my man.
 Mercutio. But I'll be hanged, sir, if he wear your 56 livery.
Marry, go before to field, he'll be your follower! 57
Your worship in that sense may call him man. 58
 Tybalt. Romeo, the love I bear thee can afford 59
No better term than this: thou art a villain.
 Romeo. Tybalt, the reason that I have to love thee 61
Doth much excuse the appertaining rage 62
To such a greeting. Villain am I none.
Therefore farewell. I see thou knowest me not. 64
 Tybalt. Boy, this shall not excuse the injuries 65
That thou hast done me; therefore turn and draw.
 Romeo. I do protest I never injured thee,
But love thee better than thou canst devise 68
Till thou shalt know the reason of my love;
And so, good Capulet, which name I tender
As dearly as mine own, be satisfied.
 Mercutio. O calm, dishonorable, vile submission!

Alla stoccata carries it away.   [*Draws.* 73
Tybalt, you ratcatcher, will you walk? 74
 Tybalt. What wouldst thou have with me?
 Mercutio. Good King of Cats, nothing but one of your nine lives. That I mean to make bold withal, and, as 77
you shall use me hereafter, dry-beat the rest of the 78
eight. Will you pluck your sword out of his pilcher 79
by the ears? Make haste, lest mine be about your
ears ere it be out.
 Tybalt. I am for you.   [*Draws.* 81
 Romeo. Gentle Mercutio, put thy rapier up.
 Mercutio. Come, sir, your passado! [*They fight.* 83
 Romeo. Draw, Benvolio; beat down their weapons.
Gentlemen, for shame! forbear this outrage!
Tybalt, Mercutio, the Prince expressly hath
Forbid this bandying in Verona streets. 87
Hold Tybalt! Good Mercutio!
 [TYBALT *under* ROMEO's *arm thrusts* MERCUTIO *in,
   and flies with his* Followers.
 Mercutio.   I am hurt.
A plague a both your houses! I am sped. 88
Is he gone and hath nothing? 89
 Benvolio.   What, art thou hurt?
 Mercutio. Ay, ay, a scratch, a scratch. Marry, 'tis enough.
Where is my page? Go, villain, fetch a surgeon. 92
      [*Exit* Page.
 Romeo. Courage, man. The hurt cannot be much.
 Mercutio. No, 'tis not so deep as a well, nor so wide as a church door; but 'tis enough, 'twill serve. Ask for me to-morrow, and you shall find me a grave man. I am peppered, I warrant, for this world. A 97
plague a both your houses! Zounds, a dog, a rat, a

51. "reason coldly": work out the solution without passion.

56. "wear your livery": by your manservant.

57. "field"": battleground.

58. "Your worship": said with great sarcasm.

59. "love": used ironically, because Tybalt thinks Romeo is a villain. "afford": allow.

61. "the reason . . . thee": his marriage to one of Tybalt's family.

62. "excuse the appertaining rage...": excuse me from the rage which would become such a greeting.

64. "knowest me not": dost not know my feelings towards you.

65. "Boy": here a term of contempt. "injuries": insults (by coming to the mask uninvited—as Tybalt thinks).

68. "devise": make out, imagine.

73. "Alla stoccata carries it away": the sword gets away with it. (Alla stoccata is Italian for with the stoccado; the stoccado is a thrust in fencing).

74. "ratcatcher": because he has a name often given to cats. "will you walk?": to a quiet place where we may fight a duel.

77. "make bold withal": take, make free with.

78. "as you shall use me hereafter": according to the way in which you treat me after I have taken one of your nine lives, i.e., the way I feel after fighting with you. "dry-beat": beat hard without drawing blood (liquid).

79. "his pilcher": its case, scabbard. "ears": hilt. "By the ears" was a contemptuous expression in Shakespeare's day.

81. "for": ready for.

83. "passado": forward thrust with the sword, one foot being advanced at the same time (pas, Fr. footstep).

87. "bandying": exchanging blows.

88. "sped": finished with.

89. "hath nothing": is unhurt.

92. "villain": affectionate use of the term among friends.

97. "peppered": done for.

ROMEO AND JULIET

ACT III SCENE I

Mercutio lies dying on the ground, while Tybalt and his gang flee. He blames Romeo's interference for Tybalt's escaping unhurt. Romeo is mortified with shame at his friend's death, and its consequences. He realizes that worse is to come, and, when Tybalt reenters, Romeo throws family consideration to the winds, engages Tybalt in a duel, and kills him. The citizens rush up, and Benvolio tells Romeo to flee. Benvolio stays, and is taken before the Prince, who soon arrives, accompanied by Lord Montague and Lord Capulet and their wives and servants.

mouse, a cat, to scratch a man to death! a braggart, a rogue, a villain, that fights by the book of arithme- 100
tic! Why the devil came you between us? I was hurt under your arm.

Romeo. I thought all for the best.

Mercutio. Help me into some house, Benvolio,
Or I shall faint. A plague a both your houses!
They have made worms' meat of me. I have it, 105
And soundly too. Your houses!

                        [*Exit, supported by* BENVOLIO.

Romeo. This gentleman, the Prince's near ally, 107
My very friend, hath got this mortal hurt 108
In my behalf—my reputation stained
With Tybalt's slander—Tybalt, that an hour 110
Hath been my cousin. O sweet Juliet,
Thy beauty hath made me effeminate
And in my temper soft'ned valor's steel! 113

            Enter BENVOLIO.

Benvolio. O Romeo, Romeo, brave Mercutio is dead!
That gallant spirit hath aspired the clouds, 115
Which too untimely here did scorn the earth.

Romeo. This day's black fate on moe days doth de- 117
pend;
This but begins the woe others must end. 118

            Enter TYBALT.

Benvolio. Here comes the furious Tybalt back again.

Romeo. Alive in triumph, and Mercutio slain?
Away to heaven respective lenity, 121
And fire-eyed fury be my conduct now! 122
Now, Tybalt, take the 'villain' back again 123
That late thou gavest me; for Mercutio's soul
Is but a little way above our heads,
Staying for thine to keep him company.
Either thou or I, or both, must go with him.

Tybalt. Thou, wretched boy, that didst consort him here,
Shalt with him hence.

Romeo.   This shall determine that.

           They fight. TYBALT *falls.*

Benvolio. Romeo, away, be gone!
The citizens are up, and Tybalt slain. 131
Stand not amazed. The Prince will doom thee death 132
If thou art taken. Hence, be gone, away!

Romeo. O, I am fortune's fool! 134

Benvolio.   Why dost thou stay?

                 [*Exit* ROMEO.

        Enter Citizens.

Citizen. Which way ran he that killed Mercutio?
Tybalt, that murderer, which way ran he?

Benvolio. There lies that Tybalt.

Citizen.   Up, sir, go with me.
I charge thee in the Prince's name obey.

Enter PRINCE [*attended*], *old* MONTAGUE, CAPULET,
        their Wives, *and all.*

Prince. Where are the vile beginners of this fray?

Benvolio. O noble Prince, I can discover all
The unlucky manage of this fatal brawl. 141
There lies the man, slain by young Romeo,
That slew thy kinsman, brave Mercutio.

100. "by the book of arithmetic": according to a set plan. Mercutio has previously said in his fighting Tybalt, he "keeps time, distance, and proportion."

105. "I have it": I've had it.

107. "ally": kinsman.

108. "very": (adjective) true.

110. "With Tybalt's slander": "Thou art a villain."

113. "temper": temperament, punning on the "temper" of steel.

115. "aspired": soared to, risen to.

117. "on moe days doth depend": hangs over other days (in the future).

118. "others": other woes.

121. "respective lenity": lenity that respects the difference between persons.

122. "conduct": guide.

123. "take the 'villain' back again": take back the word 'villain'.

131. "up": in arms, in a rabble.

132. "amazed": stupefied.

134. "fortune's fool": the plaything of luck.

141. "manage": course or management.

ROMEO AND JULIET

ACT III SCENE I

The Prince asks for full details of this affair, and Benvolio explains Romeo's reluctance to fight, and accuses the dead Tybalt for starting it all. Lady Capulet defends Tybalt, her favorite nephew, and claims that Benvolio is lying to protect Romeo, since they are "both Montagues."

The Prince weighs the evidence, and leniently decides to banish Romeo from the city. Each family also has to pay a heavy fine, subject to no appeal. Romeo will be put to death if he is henceforth found inside the walls of the city. Tybalt's body is removed as the Prince departs.

This scene achieves the following dramatic purposes:

1. It contains the crisis, or turning point.

2. It contains two spectacular street fights, and finally unites the antagonistic elements of the two rival houses in a common judgement.

3. The rapidity of events and the various moods hold the audience in suspense.

4. It further complicates Romeo's love story, and deepens our sympathy for him to the level of pity.

Capulet's Wife. Tybalt, my cousin! O my brother's child!
O Prince! O husband! O, the blood is spilled
Of my dear kinsman! Prince, as thou art true,
For blood of ours shed blood of Montague.
O cousin, cousin!
 Prince. Benvolio, who began this bloody fray?
 Benvolio. Tybalt, here slain, whom Romeo's hand did slay.
Romeo, that spoke him fair, bid him bethink
How nice the quarrel was, and urgal withal 152
Your high displeasure. All this—uttered
With gentle breath, calm look, knees humbly bowed—
Could not take truce with the unruly spleen 155
Of Tybalt deaf to peace, but that he tilts 156
With piercing steel at bold Mercutio's breast;
Who, all as hot, turns deadly point to point, 158
And, with a martial scorn, with one hand beats
Cold death aside and with the other sends 160
It back to Tybalt, whose dexterity
Retorts it. Romeo he cries aloud, 162
'Hold, friends! friends, part!' and swifter than his tongue,
His agile arm beats down their fatal points,
And 'twixt them rushes; underneath whose arm
An envious thrust from Tybalt hit the life 166
Of stout Mercutio, and then Tybalt fled;
But by and by comes back to Romeo,
Who had but newly entertained revenge, 169
And to't they go like lightning; for, ere I
Could draw to part them, was stout Tybalt slain;
And, as he fell, did Romeo turn and fly.
This is the truth, or let Benvolio die.
 Capulet's Wife. He is a kinsman to the Montague;
Affection makes him false, he speaks not true.
Some twenty of them fought in this black strife,
And all those twenty could but kill one life.
I beg for justice, which thou, Prince, must give.
Romeo slew Tybalt; Romeo must not live.
 Prince. Romeo slew him; he slew Mercutio.
Who now the price of his dear blood doth owe? 181
 Montague. Not Romeo, Prince; he was Mercutio's friend;
His fault concludes but what the law should end, 183
The life of Tybalt.
 Prince.   And for that offense
Immediately we do exile him hence.
I have an interest in your hate's proceeding, 186
My blood for your rude brawls doth lie a-bleeding; 187
But I'll amerce you with so strong a fine 188
That you shall all repent the loss of mine.
I will be deaf to pleading and excuses;
Nor tears nor prayers shall purchase out abuses. 191
Therefore use none. Let Romeo hence in haste,
Else, when he is found, that hour is his last.
Bear hence this body, and attend our will. 194
Mercy but murders. pardoning those that kill. 195
        [*Exit, with others.*

152. "nice": trivial.
 "withal": in addition, thereto.

155. "unruly spleen"; uncontrolled anger.

156. "but that he tilts": so that he should NOT tilt (tilt—thrust AT).

158. "hot": hot-tempered.

160. "Cold death": Tybalt's sword.

162. "Retorts it": turns it back.

166. "envious": spiteful, malicious.

169. "newly entertained": recently thought of.

181. "Who now the price of his dear blood doth owe?": who must pay for Tybalt's death?

183. "concludes": brings to an end (by killing).

186. "your hate's proceeding": the consequences of your feud.

187. "My blood": Mercutio was the Prince's kinsman.

188. "amerce": punish.

191. "purchase out": buy a pardon for.

194. "attend our will": wait on "us" to do what "we" require, or, perhaps, pay attention to what "we" have decided.

195. "Mercy . . . kill": giving pardon to murderer only causes more murders to take place.

ROMEO AND JULIET

ACT III SCENE II

The young bride waits impatiently in her father's orchard for the coming of night, of Romeo, and the consummation of their marriage. The speech beginning "Gallop apace, you fiery-footed steeds . . . " expresses in a masterly way the impatience of her desire. This speech constitutes Juliet's PROTHALAMION, or bridal song in which she looks forward to physical union with her lover. Alas! there will be little occasion for an EPITHALAMION! This soliloquy is unrhymed so that it moves with a spontaneous impetus in keeping with the young girl's exalted mood. Once again, Shakespeare demonstrates his superb ability to match the structural form to the atmospherics of mood and other content with felicitous exactitude.

Scene two.

(THE SAME. CAPULET'S ORCHARD)

Enter JULIET *alone.*

Juliet. Gallop apace, you fiery-footed steeds,   1
Towards Phoebus' lodging! Such a wagoner   2
As Phaeton would whip you to the west   3
And bring in cloudy night immediately.
Spread thy close curtain, love-performing night,   5
That runaways' eyes may wink, and Romeo   6
Leap to these arms untalked of and unseen.
Lovers can see to do their amorous rites
By their own beauties; or, if love be blind,
It best agrees with night. Come. civil night,   10
Thou sober-suited matron, all in black,
And learn me how to lose a winning match,   12
Played for a pair of stainless maidenhoods.
Hood my unmanned blood, bating in my cheeks,   14
With thy black mantle till strange love grow bold,   15
Think true love acted simple modesty.
Come, night; come, Romeo; come, thou day in night;   17
For thou wilt lie upon the wings of night
Whiter than new snow upon a raven's back.
Come, gentle night; come, loving, black-browed
    night;
Give me my Romeo; and, when he shall die,   21
Take him and cut him out in little stars,
And he will make the face of heaven so fine   23
That all the world will be in love with night
And pay no worship to the garish sun.   25
O, I have bought the mansion of a love,
But not possessed it; and though I am sold,   27
Not yet enjoyed. So tedious is this day
As is the night before some festival
To an impatient child that hath new robes
And may not wear them. O. here comes my nurse,

Enter Nurse, *with cords.*

And she brings news; and every tongue that speaks
But Romeo's name speaks heavenly eloquence.
Now, nurse, what news? What hast thou there, the
    cords
That Romeo bid thee fetch?
Nurse.   Ay. ay, the cords.
                    [*Throws them down.*
Juliet. Ay me! what news? Why dost thou wring
    thy hands?
Nurse. Ah, weraday! he's dead, he's dead, he's   37
    dead!
We are undone, lady, we are undone!
Alack the day! he's gone, he's killed, he's dead!
Juliet. Can heaven be so envious?
Nurse.   Romeo can,
Though heaven cannot. O Romeo, Romeo!
Who ever would have thought it? Romeo!
Juliet. What devil art thou that dost torment me
    thus?

1. "steeds": horses (of the sun).

2. "Phoebus": sun-god.
"wagoner": driver.

3. "Phaeton": son of Helios (the sun) who tried for one day to drive his father's chariot; he so nearly set the earth on fire that Zeus had to strike him dead with a thunderbolt.

5. "love-performing": making it easy for lovers.

6. "wink": close, be unable to see.

10. "civil": sober, serious.

12. "lose a winning match": gain, by surrendering, a husband for myself.

14. "Hood my unmanned blood": a metaphor from falconry. There is a pun on unmanned."

15. "strange": unfamiliar, reserved.

17. "day": bright joy.

21. "when he shall die": surely Juliet would not think of Romeo's death now! The implication is that when she is gone she does not want any other women to enjoy him, but "all the world."

23. "fine": bright.

25. "garish": too bright; therefore, tawdry.

27. "I am sold": continuing the metaphor of the empty house in reverse. She has sold herself to Romeo, but he has not yet entered into possession.

37. "weraday": a corruption of an Old English exclamation of woe. Similar to "alas the day" (an intensified form of "alas"), I. 72, and "alack the day," IV. v. 22.

ROMEO AND JULIET

ACT III SCENE II

The nurse enters, wringing her hands and, by her vague words, suggests erroneously that Romeo is dead — not merely banished. Juliet asks what devil she has to torment her thus, then learns that Tybalt is dead. From this she concludes they are both, the only men for whom she cared, dead. The nurse eventually tells her what the actual situation is, and Juliet denounces Romeo as a "serpent heart, hid with a flowering face!" The nurse joins her mistress by denouncing men; "There's no trust,/ No faith, no honesty in men." She immediately disqualifies these all-inclusive sentiments by calling for her "man," i.e., her servant,

---

This torture should be roared in dismal hell.
Hath Romeo slain himself? Say thou but 'I,' 45
And that bare vowel 'I' shall poison more
Than the death-darting eye of cockatrice. 47
I am not I, if there be such an 'I'
Or those eyes shut that makes the answer 'I.' 49
If he be slain, say 'I'; or if not, 'no.'
Brief sounds determine of my weal or woe. 51
   Nurse. I saw the wound, I saw it with mine eyes,
(God save the mark!) here on his manly breast. 53
A piteous corse, a bloody piteous corse; 54
Pale, pale as ashes, all bedaubed in blood,
All in gore-blood. I swounded at the sight. 56
   Juliet. O, break, my heart! poor bankrout, break 57
     at once!
To prison, eyes; ne'er look on liberty!
Vile earth, to earth resign; end motion here, 59
And thou and Romeo press one heavy bier! 60
   Nurse. O Tybalt, Tybalt, the best friend I had!
O courteous Tybalt! honest gentleman!
That ever I should live to see thee dead!
   Juliet. What storm is this that blows so contrary? 64
Is Romeo slaught'red, and is Tybalt dead?
My dearest cousin, and my dearer lord?
Then, dreadful trumpet, sound the general doom! 67
For who is living, if those two are gone?
   Nurse. Tybalt is gone, and Romeo banished;
Romeo that killed him, he is banished;
   Juliet. O God! Did Romeo's hand shed Tybalt's
     blood?
   Nurse. It did, it did! alas the day, it did!
   Juliet. O serpent heart, hid with a flow'ring face! 73
Did ever dragon keep so fair a cave?
Beautiful tyrant! fiend angelical!
Dove-feathered raven! wolvish-ravening lamb!
Despised substance of divinest show! 77
Just opposite to what thou justly seem'st— 78
A damned saint, an honorable villain!
O nature, what hadst thou to do in hell 80
When thou didst bower the spirit of a fiend 81
In mortal paradise of such sweet flesh?
Was ever book containing such vile matter
So fairly bound? O, that deceit should dwell
In such a gorgeous palace!
   Nurse.   There's no trust,
No faith, no honesty in men; all perjured,
All forsworn, all naught, all dissemblers. 87
Ah, where's my man? Give me some aqua vitae.
These griefs, these woes, these sorrows make me old.
Shame come to Romeo!
   Juliet.   Blistered be thy tongue
For such a wish! He was not born to shame.
Upon his brow shame is ashamed to sit;
For 'tis a throne where honor may be crowned
Sole monarch of the universal earth.
O, what a beast was I to chide at him!
   Nurse. Will you speak well of him that killed your
     cousin?
   Juliet. Shall I speak ill of him that is my husband?
Ah, poor my lord, what tongue shall smooth thy 98
     name

---

45. " 'I' ": the affirmative 'Ay,' which was spelled 'I' in the Elizabethan age.

47. "cockatrice": a creature fabled to kill by a look, said to be like a serpent with a cock's head; often identified with the basilisk.

49. "Or those eyes shut that make thee answer 'I' ": or if (Romeo's) eyes be shut . . .

51. "Brief sounds determine of": let brief sounds decide.
"weal": welfare.

53. "God save the mark!": pardon me for saying it!

54. "corse": corpse.

56. "gore": coagulated.

57. "bankrout": Juliet's investment in Romeo has come to naught.

59. "Vile earth": addressing her own body.
"resign": submit (reflexive).

60. "heavy": because it has the weight of two bodies.

64. "so contrary": in opposite directions.

67. "general doom": reference to the day of wrath at the end of the world (St. Paul: I Corinthians, XV, 52).

73. "serpent . . . face!": like a serpent under a flower, a comparison Shakespeare uses again in Macbeth.

77. "divinest show": excellent appearance.

78. "Just": exactly.
"justly": rightly.

80. "hadst thou to do": were you about.

81. "bower": enclose, contain in a bower, embower.

87. "naught": worthless, good-for-nothing.
"dissemblers": liars.

98. "smooth": speak well of (with a pun on the literal meaning as opposed to 'mangled' in the following line).

ROMEO AND JULIET

ACT III SCENE II

to give her some reviving cognac (aqua vitae). She hopes shame will come to Romeo. This wish has the effect of making Juliet rush to the defense of the man who is now, despite all, her own husband. She rebukes both her nurse and herself for chiding Romeo, and weeps at the recollection of the sin she has so recently committed.

Suddenly remembering Romeo's exile, she sees the rope ladder languishing, unerected, on the floor, and addresses the ropes in a piteous apostrophe:

Poor ropes, you are beguiled, Both you and I, for Romeo is exiled:

He made you for a highway to my bed,

But I, a maid, die maiden-widowed.

Come, cords; come nurse; I'll take to my wedding bed:

And death, not Romeo, take my maidenhead.

The nurse tells Juliet to hasten to her room; she knows where Romeo is hiding, at Friar Laurence's cell, and will see that he visits Juliet here tonight.

The dramatic purposes achieved by this scene are:

1. It shows how Juliet receives the bad news.

2. It adds an element of unbearable suspense and grim humor to the retelling of the news by the incompetent and circumlocutory nurse.

3. It shows Juliet's warmth and humanity, not merely her ecstatic happiness.

4. The only meeting of Romeo and Juliet AFTER their marriage is arranged here — the "highway" to her bed.

ACT III SCENE III

Romeo awaits news of his sentence at Friar Laurence's cell, that place which, a few hours earlier, had witnessed his nuptial meeting with his bride. How different are his emotions now! Friar Laurence announces the verdict,

---

When I, thy three-hours wife, have mangled it?
But wherefore, villain, didst thou kill my cousin?
That villain cousin would have killed my husband. 101
Back, foolish tears, back to your native spring!
Your tributary drops belong to woe,
Which you, mistaking, offer up to joy.
My husband lives, that Tybalt would have slain;
And Tybalt's dead, that would have slain my husband.
All this is comfort; wherefore weep I then?
Some word there was, worser than Tybalt's death,
That murd'red me. I would forget it fain;
But O, it presses to my memory 110
Like damned guilty deeds to sinners' minds!
'Tybalt is dead, and Romeo—banished.'
That 'banished,' that one word 'banished,'
Hath slain ten thousand Tybalts. Tybalt's death 114
Was woe enough, if it had ended there;
Or, if sour woe delights in fellowship
And needly will be ranked with other griefs,
Why followed not, when she said 'Tybalt's dead,'
Thy father, or thy mother, nay, or both, 119
Which modern lamentation might have moved? 120
But with a rearward following Tybalt's death,
'Romeo is banished'—to speak that word
Is father, mother, Tybalt, Romeo, Juliet, 123
All slain, all dead. 'Romeo is banished'—
There is no end, no limit, measure, bound,
In that word's death; no words can that woe sound. 126
Where is my father and my mother, nurse?
  Nurse. Weeping and wailing over Tybalt's corse.
Will you go to them? I will bring you thither.
  Juliet. Wash they his wounds with tears? Mine
    shall be spent, 130
When theirs are dry, for Romeo's banishment.
Take up those cords. Poor ropes, you are beguiled, 132
Both you and I, for Romeo is exiled.
He made you for a highway to my bed;
But I a maid, die maiden-widowed.
Come, cords; come, nurse. I'll to my wedding bed; 136
And death, not Romeo, take my maidenhead!
  Nurse. Hie to your chamber. I'll find Romeo
To comfort you. I wot well where he is. 139
Hark ye, your Romeo will be here at night.
I'll to him; he is hid at Laurence' cell.
  Juliet. O, find him! give this ring to my true knight
And bid him come to take his last farewell.
                [*Exit with* Nurse.

Scene three.

(THE SAME. FRIAR LAURENCE'S CELL)

Enter FRIAR LAURENCE.

  Friar. Romeo, come forth; come forth, thou fearful
    man. 1
Affliction is enamored of thy parts, 2
And thou art wedded to calamity.

---

101. "That villain . . . husband": her intuition gives her the answer to her own question.

110. "presses to": forces itself on.

114. "Hath slain": on balance is equal to the death of.

119. "Thy": i.e., Juliet's.

120. "modern": common (NOT up-to-date!).

123. "Is": is equal to.

126. "that word's": the word "banished." "sound": utter, or plumb the depth of.

130. "spent": shed (NOT exhausted!).

132. "beguiled": cheated (of your purpose).

136. "I'll to my wedding bed": Cf. her speech near the end of I. v.—"My grave is like to be my wedding bed."

139. "wot": know.

1. "fearful": frightened (as to what is about to happen to him).

2. "enamored of": in love with. "parts": good qualities (as in the expression 'a man of parts').

52

ACT III SCENE III

"Not body's death, but body's banishment." Romeo fears exile more than execution, because "there is no world without Verona walls."

The Friar condemns Romeo's unconstructive and sinful attitude, but Romeo is too upset and, after making a tirade against banishment, sinks onto the floor in distress.

Enter ROMEO.

Romeo. Father, what news? What is the Prince's
  doom?   4
What sorrow craves acquaintance at my hand
That I yet know not?
Friar.   Too familiar
Is my dear son with such sour company.
I bring thee tidings of the Prince's doom.
Romeo. What less than doomsday is the Prince's
  doom?
Friar. A gentler judgment vanished from his lips— 10
Not body's death, but body's banishment.
Romeo. Ha, banishment? Be merciful, say 'death';
For exile hath more terror in his look,
Much more than death. Do not say 'banishment.'
Friar. Hence from Verona art thou banished.
Be patient, for the world is broad and wide.
Romeo. There is no world without Verona walls,
But purgatory, torture, hell itself.
Hence banished is banished from the world,
And world's exile is death. Then 'banished'   20
Is death mistermed. Calling death 'banished,'
Thou cut'st my head off with a golden axe   22
And smilest upon the stroke that murders me.
Friar. O deadly sin! O rude unthankfulness!
Thy fault our law calls death; but the kind Prince, 25
Taking thy part, hath rushed aside the law,   26
And turned that black word 'death' to banishment.
This is dear mercy, and thou seest it not.   28
Romeo. 'Tis torture, and not mercy. Heaven is here,
Where Juliet lives; and every cat and dog
And little mouse, every unworthy thing,
Live here in heaven and may look on her;
But Romeo may not. More validity,
More honorable state, more courtship lives   34
In carrion flies than Romeo. They may seize
On the white wonder of dear Juliet's hand
And steal immortal blessing from her lips,
Who, even in pure and vestal modesty,
Still blush, as thinking their own kisses sin;
But Romeo may not, he is banished.
Flies may do this but I from this must fly;
They are freemen, but I am banished.
And sayest thou yet that exile is not death?
Hadst thou no poison mixed, no sharp-ground knife,
No sudden mean of death, though ne'er so mean
But 'banished' to kill me—'banished'?
O friar, the damned use that word in hell;
Howling attends it! How hast thou the heart,
Being a divine, ghostly confessor,
A sin-absolver, and my friend professed,
To mangle me with that word 'banished'?
Friar. Thou fond mad man, hear me a little speak. 52
Romeo. O, thou wilt speak again of banishment.
Friar. I'll give thee armor to keep off that word; 54
Adversity's sweet milk, philosophy,   55
To comfort thee, though thou art banished.
Romeo. Yet 'banished'? Hang up philosophy!   57
Unless philosophy can make a Juliet,
Displant a town, reverse a prince's doom,

4. "doom": judgment (passed on me).

10. "vanished": came forth.

20. "world's exile": Romeo feels exiled from the world.

22. "with a golden axe": you call it by a more attractive name, but the effect is just as deadly.

25. "death": as a punishment.

26. "rushed aside": pushed aside.

28. "dear mercy": loving mercy.

34. "courtship": state suitable to a court (carries also the notion of a lover's courting a mistress).

52. "fond": foolish.

54. "armor": protection (in the form of philosophic resignation, or stoicism).

55. "sweet milk": it makes adversity palatable.

57. "Hang up": get rid of (as the hangman gets rid of a criminal).

It helps not, it prevails not. Talk no more.

Friar. O, then I see that madmen have no ears.

Romeo. How should they, when that wise men have no eyes?

Friar. Let me dispute with thee of thy estate. 63

Romeo. Thou canst not speak of that thou dost not feel.

Wert thou as young as I, Juliet thy love,

An hour but married, Tybalt murdered,

Doting like me, and like me banished, 67

Then mightst thou speak, then mightst thou tear thy hair,

And fall upon the ground, as I do now,

Taking the measure of an unmade grave.

            [*Enter* Nurse *and knock.*

Friar. Arise; one knocks. Good Romeo, hide thyself.

Romeo. Not I; unless the breath of heartsick groans

Mist-like infold me from the search of eyes. [*Knock.* 73

Friar. Hark, how they knock! Who's there? Romeo, rise;

Thou wilt be taken.—Stay awhile!—Stand up;

            [*Knock.*

Run to my study.—By and by!—God's will,

What simpleness is this.—I come, I come! [*Knock.* 77

Who knocks so hard? Whence come you? What's your will?

          Enter Nurse.

Nurse. Let me come in, and you shall know my errand.

I come from Lady Juliet.

Friar.   Welcome then.

Nurse. O holy friar, O, tell me, holy friar,

Where is my lady's lord, where's Romeo?

Friar. There on the ground, with his own tears made drunk.

Nurse. O, he is even in my mistress' case, 84

Just in her case! O woeful sympathy! 85

Piteous predicament! Even so lies she, 86

Blubb'ring and weeping, weeping and blubb'ring.

Stand up, stand up! Stand, an you be a man.

For Juliet's sake, for her sake, rise and stand!

Why should you fall into so deep an O? 90

Romeo. [*rises*] Nurse—

Nurse. Ah sir! ah sir! Death's the end of all.

Romeo. Spakest thou of Juliet? How is it with her?

Doth not she think me an old murderer, 94

Now I have stained the childhood of our joy

With blood removed but little from her own?

Where is she? and how doth she! and what says

My concealed lady to our cancelled love? 98

Nurse. O, she says nothing, sir, but weeps and weeps;

And now falls on her bed, and then starts up,

And Tybalt calls; and then on Romeo cries,

And then down falls again.

Romeo.   As if that name,

Shot from the deadly level of a gun, 103

Did murder her; as that name's cursed hand

Murdered her kinsman. O, tell me, friar, tell me,

A knocking at the door heralds the nurse, who comes with a message from Juliet. She finds Romeo in a "piteous predicament," like Juliet, "blubbering and weeping, weeping and blubbering."

63. "estate": condition.

67. "Doting": passionately in love.

73. "infold me": enfold me, wrap me up.

77. "simpleness": folly.

84. "case": position.

85. "sympathy": identification (empathy) in suffering.

86. "predicament": Juliet's condition.

90. "O": groan, lament.

94. "old": seasoned.

98. "My concealed lady": Juliet, who is not known to most others as my wife.

103. "level": aim.

ROMEO AND JULIET

ACT III SCENE III

At one point Romeo draws his sword and, in despair, threatens to kill himself, but the holy friar prevents this, and in the longest speech in the play (51 lines) attempts to explain the situation. Friar Laurence makes the following points:

(a) Romeo must play the man.

(b) Does he wish to slay Juliet by murdering himself?

(c) He disgraces both his good sense and his vows.

(d) He still is married to Juliet.

(e) He won the duel.

(f) Banishment is better than death.

(g) He should look at his blessings, not ignore them.

(h) He should now go to Juliet and stay with her.

(i) But he should not stay until the Watch comes on duty.

(j) Then he should leave for the neighboring city of Mantua.

(k) He will remain there until such time as he earns pardon from the Prince.

Friar Laurence's calm voice and clear reasoning revived Romeo; the nurse is delighted by the sermon—"O, what learing is!"—and gives Romeo Juliet's ring and asks him to hurry back to Juliet's room with her. Much encouraged, Romeo hurries off to consummate the marriage. We recall the Friar's previous premonitions; were they, after all, unjustified?

This scene fulfils the following dramatic purposes:

1. It provides an opportunity for the two lovers to become 'incorporated' in fact, as well as in law.

2. It arranges for Romeo to go twenty miles to neighboring Mantua to serve his period of exile.

3. It offers two conceptions of banishment for comparison.

4. The friar's long speech is both a DIAGNOSIS and a PROGNOSIS of Romeo's case, with whose romantic AETIOLOGY we are already familiar.

In what vile part of this anatomy
Doth my name lodge? Tell me, that I may sack
The hateful mansion.

[*He offers to stab himself, and
Nurse snatches the dagger away.*

Friar.   Hold thy desperate hand.
Art thou a man? Thy form cries out thou art;
Thy tears are womanish, thy wild acts denote
The unreasonable fury of a beast.
Unseemly woman in a seeming man! 112
And ill-beseeming beast in seeming both! 113
Thou hast amazed me. By my holy order,
I thought thy disposition better tempered.
Hast thou slain Tybalt? Wilt thou slay thyself?
And slay thy lady that in thy life lives,
By doing damned hate upon thyself? 118
Why railest thou on thy birth, the heaven, and earth? 119
Since birth and heaven and earth, all three do meet 120
In thee at once; which thou at once wouldst lose.
Fie, fie, thou shamest thy shape, thy love, thy wit,
Which, like a usurer, abound'st in all, 123
And usest none in that true use indeed
Which should bedeck thy shape, thy love, thy wit.
Thy noble shape is but a form of wax, 126
Digressing from the valor of a man; 127
Thy dear love sworn but hollow perjury,
Killing that love which thou hast vowed to cherish; 129
Thy wit, that ornament to shape and love, 130
Misshapen in the conduct of them both, 131
Like powder in a skilless soldier's flask,
Is set afire by thine own ignorance,
And thou dismemb'red with thine own defense. 134
What, rouse thee, man! Thy Juliet is alive,
For whose dear sake thou wast but lately dead. 136
There art thou happy. Tybalt would kill thee,
But thou slewest Tybalt. There art thou happy too.
The law, that threat'ned death, becomes thy friend
And turns it to exile. There art thou happy.
A pack of blessings light upon thy back;
Happiness courts thee in her best array;
But, like a misbehaved and sullen wench,
Thou pout'st upon thy fortune and thy love. 144
Take heed, take heed, for such die miserable.
Go get thee to thy love, as was decreed,
Ascend her chamber, hence and comfort her. 147
But look thou stay not till the watch be set,
For then thou canst not pass to Mantua.
Where thou shalt live till we can find a time
To blaze your marriage, reconcile your friends, 151
Beg pardon of the Prince, and call thee back
With twenty hundred thousand times more joy
Than thou went'st forth in lamentation.
Go before, nurse. Commend me to thy lady,
And bid her hasten all the house to bed,
Which heavy sorrow makes them apt unto. 157
Romeo is coming.

Nurse. O Lord, I could have stayed here all the
   night
To hear good counsel. O, what learning is!
My lord, I'll tell my lady you will come.

112. "Unseemly": unseemly in a man.

113. "both": a man in form and a woman in the way you take misfortune.

118. "damned hate": self-murder as an act of hatred.

119. "Why railest thou on thy birth": Romeo has not done so, but the Romeus of Brooke's poem did, and Shakespeare has here followed his source inconsistently with his play.

120-21. "meet in thee at once": have a place in you at the same time, "heaven and earth" here meaning soul and body.

123. "which abound'st in all": all of which abound in you.

123-4. "userer . . . usest . . . use": alliterative pun.

126. "but a form of wax": no more durable than a figure cast in wax.

127. "Digressing": if you depart.

129. "love": loved one, i.e., he would kill Juliet (metaphorically speaking) by his own death.

130. "that ornament": it is well-suited to his "shape (form) and love."

131. "conduct": ruling, governance.

134. "dismemb'red with": torn to pieces by.

136. "dead": ready to die.

144. "pout'st upon": treat with contempt.

147. "Ascend": it had been arranged that he should ascend to Juliet's room by a rope-ladder.

151. "blaze": proclaim.

157. "heavy sorrow": on account of Tybalt's death.

ACT III SCENE IV

Scene IV provides a change of pace; later on the evening of the same day (Monday), while Juliet is in Romeo's arms in her room upstairs, Lord and Lady Capulet are having a serious talk with Paris downstairs. Lord Capulet apologizes for the fact that he has been unable to inform Juliet of her proposed marriage to Count Paris, owing to the confusion consequent upon the killing of their relative, Tybalt.

Paris is on the point of leaving, when Lady Capulet says she will interview Juliet now, and tell her of their decision. Lord Capulet says this will not be necessary—"I think she will be ruled. In all respects by me; nay, more, I doubt it not." The re-introduction of the Paris-Juliet theme (Juliet was introduced to it in Act I, Scene III, line 63 et seq.,) as something to be realized soon gives a greater sense of urgency to the position of the lovers, especially since (unknown to Juliet!) the wedding date has been set for next Thursday. Only a few close friends will participate, owing to the mourning for Tybalt. Capulet instructs Lady Capulet to go and tell Juliet of his arrangement at once.

The dramatic purposes of this scene are:

1. A slower pace than either that of the previous or following scenes is provided here.

2. The parent-projected Paris-Juliet theme complicates the FAIT-ACCOMPLI of the Juliet-Romeo theme. (MARRIAGE DE CONVENANCE V. MARRIAGE D'AMOUR.)

3. The date of Thursday (rather than Paris' preferred date, Tuesday) allows time for Juliet's plans to be carried out.

Romeo. Do so, and bid my sweet prepare to chide. 162
Nurse. Here is a ring she bid me give you, sir.
Hie you, make haste, for it grows very late. [*Exit.*
Romeo. How well my comfort is revived by this! 165
Friar. Go hence; good night; and here stands all 166
 your state:
Either be gone before the watch be set,
Or by the break of day disguised from hence.
Sojourn in Mantua. I'll find out your man,
And he shall signify from time to time
Every good hap to you that chances here.
Give me thy hand. 'Tis late. Farewell; good night.
Romeo. But that a joy past joy calls out on me,
It were a grief so brief to part with thee.
Farewell.   [*Exeunt.*

Scene four.

(THE SAME. A ROOM IN CAPULET'S HOUSE)

Enter old CAPULET, *his* Wife, *and* PARIS.

Capulet. Things have fall'n out, sir, so unluckily
That we have had no time to move our daughter. 2
Look you, she loved her kinsman Tybalt dearly,
And so did I. Well, we were born to die.
'Tis very late; she'll not come down to-night.
I promise you, but for your company,
I would have been abed an hour ago.
Paris. These times of woe afford no times to woo.
Madam, good night. Commend me to your daughter.
Lady. I will, and know her mind early to-morrow; 10
To-night she's mewed up to her heaviness. 11
Capulet. Sir Paris, I will make a desperate tender 12
Of my child's love. I think she will be ruled
In all respects by me; nay more, I doubt it not.
Wife, go you to her ere you go to bed;
Acquaint her here of my son Paris' love
And bid her (mark you me?) on Wednesday next—
But soft! what day is this?
Paris.   Monday, my lord.
Capulet. Monday! ha, ha! Well, Wednesday is too
 soon. 19
A Thursday let it be—a Thursday, tell her,
She shall be married to this noble earl.
Will you be ready? Do you like this haste?
We'll keep no great ado—a friend or two; 23
For hark you, Tybalt being slain so late,
It may be thought we held him carelessly, 25
Being our kinsman, if we revel much.
Therefore we'll have some half a dozen friends,
And there an end. But what say you to Thursday?
Paris. My lord, I would that Thursday were to-
 morrow.
Capulet. Well, get you gone. A Thursday be it then.
Go you to Juliet ere you go to bed;
Prepare her, wife, against this wedding day.
Farewell, my lord.—Light to my chamber, ho!

162. "to chide": to rebuke.

165. "How well . . . this!": the fact that Juliet has sent him a ring shows that she still loves him although he has slain her kinsman.

166. "here stands all your state": your entire future depends on this.

2. "move": persuade, sway.

10. "know": find out, discover.

11. "mewed up to her heaviness": encaged in her grief.

12. "desperate tender": bold offer.

19. "ha,ha!": (NOT laughter) denotes a pause for reflection: h'm, h'm.

23. "keep no great ado": make no big fuss.

25. "held him carelessly": thought little of him.

ACT III SCENE V

It will be recalled that Romeo must leave Juliet before dawn on Tuesday morning, in order to get safely out of Verona owing to the sentence of death that hangs over him if found within the precincts of the city. Romeo is taking a lingering farewell of his newly-deflowered bride; the richness of this poetry, with ite emotive references to the lark (symbol of encroaching dawn) rather than to the nightingale (symbol of the evening that is past), recalls the passional poetry displayed previously, in the sonnet of mutual recognition and in the "Gallop apace" speech of Juliet, the anticipatory bride and lover. At the mention of "death" Juliet reluctantly lets her lover go.

The faithful though incompetent nurse enters and warns Juliet that Lady Capulet is approaching. It is clear that until now Juliet has been out on the balcony, on the upper stage. Juliet now descends to the main stage after Romeo's departure.

Afore me, it is so very very late   34
That we may call it early by and by.   35
Good night.   [*Exeunt.*

Scene five.

(THE SAME. JULIET'S CHAMBER)

Enter ROMEO *and* JULIET *aloft, at the window.*

Juliet. Wilt thou be gone? It is not yet near day.   1
It was the nightingale, and not the lark,
That pierced the fearful hollow of thine ear.   3
Nightly she sings on yond pomegranate tree.
Believe me, love, it was the nightingale.
Romeo. It was the lark, the herald of the morn;
No nightingale. Look, love, what envious streaks
Do lace the severing clouds in yonder East.
Night's candles are burnt out, and jocund day   9
Stands tiptoe on the misty mountain tops.   10
I must be gone and live, or stay and die.
Juliet. Yond light is not daylight; I know it, I.
It is some meteor that the sun exhales   13
To be to thee this night a torchbearer
And light thee on thy way to Mantua.
Therefore stay yet; thou need'st not to be gone.
Romeo. Let me be ta'en, let me be put to death.
I am content, so thou wilt have it so.   18
I'll say yon grey is not the morning's eye,
'Tis but the pale reflex of Cynthia's brow;   20
Nor that is not the lark whose notes do beat
The vaulty heaven so high above our heads.
I have more care to stay than will to go.
Come, death, and welcome! Juliet wills it so.
How is't, my soul? Let's talk; it is not day.
Juliet. It is, it is! Hie hence, be gone, away!
It is the lark that sings so out of tune,
Straining harsh discords and unpleasing sharps.
Some say the lark makes sweet division;   29
This doth not so, for she divideth us.
Some say the lark and loathed toad change eyes;   31
O, now I would they had changed voices too,   32
Since arm from arm that voice doth us affray,   33
Hunting thee hence with hunt's-up to the day.   34
O, now be gone! More light and light it grows.
Romeo. More light and light—more dark and dark
     our woes.

Enter Nurse, *hastily.*

Nurse. Madam!
Juliet. Nurse?
Nurse. Your lady mother is coming to your chamber.
The day is broke; be wary, look about.   [*Exit.*
Juliet. Then, window, let day in, and let life out.   41
Romeo. Farewell, farewell! One kiss, and I'll
     descend.   [*He goeth down.*
Juliet. Art thou gone so, love-lord, ay husband-
     friend?
I must hear from thee every day in the hour,
For in a minute there are many days.

34. "Afore me!": before me, a pretty oath, weakened from "Afore God!" He is politely telling Paris to go before him as they leave.

35. "by and by": soon.

1. "Wilt": must.

3. "fearful": sounds make him fearful because he dreads discovery by day.

9. "Night's candles": the stars.

10. "tiptoe": ready to spring forth.

13. "meteor that the sun exhales": meteors were thought to be caused by the rays of the sun igniting vapors drawn up ("exhaled") from the earth by the sun's warmth.

18. "so": if, provided that.

20. "reflex": reflection. "Cynthia's": the moon's.

29. "division": a quick run of notes.

31. "the lark . . . eyes": a rustic fancy because the toad's eyes are beautiful and the lark's small and unattractive.

32. "I would . . . too!": for the toad's croak would be not "herald of the morn."

33. "arm from arm that voice doth us affray": frighten us out of one another's arms.

34. "hunts-up": originally the sound that roused huntsmen, this expression means any morning greeting.

41. "life": Romeo.

O, by this count I shall be much in years   46
Ere I again behold my Romeo!
Romeo. Farewell!
I will omit no opportunity
That may convey my greetings, love, to thee.
Juliet. O, think'st thou we shall ever meet again?
Romeo. I doubt it not; and all these woes shall serve
For sweet discourses in our times to come.
Juliet. O God, I have an ill-divining soul!   54
Methinks I see thee, now thou art so low,
As one dead in the bottom of a tomb.
Either my eyesight fails, or thou lookest pale.
Romeo. And trust me, love, in my eye so do you.
Dry sorrow drinks our blood. Adieu, adieu!   [*Exit.*   59
Juliet. O Fortune, Fortune! all men call thee fickle.
If thou art fickle, what dost thou with him   61
That is renowned for faith? Be fickle, Fortune,
For then I hope thou wilt not keep him long
But send him back.

[She goeth down from the window.

Enter Mother.

Lady. Ho, daughter! are you up?
Juliet. Who is't that calls? It is my lady mother.
Is she not down so late, or up so early?   67
What unaccustomed cause procures her hither?   68
Lady. Why, how now, Juliet?
Juliet.   Madam, I am not well.
Lady. Evermore weeping for your cousin's death?
What, wilt thou wash him from his grave with tears?
An if thou couldst, thou couldst not make him live.
Therefore have done. Some grief shows much of love;   73
But much of grief shows still some want of wit.   74
Juliet. Yet let me weep for such a feeling loss.   75
Lady. So shall you feel the loss, but not the friend 76
Which you weep for.
Juliet.   Feeling so the loss,
I cannot choose but ever weep the friend.
Lady. Well, girl, thou weep'st not so much for his death
As that the villain lives which slaughtered him.
Juliet. What villain, madam?
Lady.   That same villain Romeo.
Juliet. [*aside*] Villain and he be many miles asunder.—
God pardon him! I do, with all my heart;
And yet no man like he doth grieve my heart.
Lady. That is because the traitor murderer lives.
Juliet. Ay, madam, from the reach of these my hands.
Would none but I might venge my cousin's death!
Lady. We will have vengeance for it, fear thou not.
Then weep no more. I'll send to one in Mantua,
Where that same banished runagate doth live,   90
Shall give him such an unaccustomed dram   91
That he shall soon keep Tybalt company;
And then I hope thou wilt be satisfied.
Juliet. Indeed I never shall be satisfied
With Romeo till I behold him—dead—   95
Is my poor heart so for a kinsman vexed.

46. "count": reckoning.
"in years": older.

54. "ill-divining": foreboding evil.

59. "dry sorrow drinks our blood": another old belief, that sorrow caused people to go pale through lack of blood.

61. "dost thou": is your concern.

67. "down": gone to bed—to lie down.

68. "procures": brings, with overtones of 'procuring' or of 'being procured.'

69. "how now": what's the matter?

73. "Some": a little.

74. "still": always.

75. "feeling": deeply felt. She really means Romeo, though she knows Lady Capulet will take it to refer to Tybalt.

76. "but not": but not feel, i.e., your grief will not bring back the friend whom you mourn.

90. "runagate": vagabond (runaway).

91. "unaccustomed dram": dram to which he is unaccustomed (poison).

95. "dead": Romeo is dead, and so is Juliet's heart.

Lady Capulet rebukes her daughter for weeping and tells Juliet the "good" news about the arranged marriage with Paris. A conversation at cross purposes ensues, in which the technique of dramatic irony is employed; the audience and Juliet realize that Lady Capulet's remarks refer to Tybalt's death, but only the audience (not Lady Capulet) realizes that Juliet's remarks refer to her grief on the departure of Romeo.

When Juliet realizes the "treat" which is in store for her at Saint Peter's church on Thursday morning, she refuses to marry Count Paris—why, he has not even troubled to court her! She refuses point-blank to marry a stranger, fearing the complication with her previously-contracted secret marriage.

Capulet and the nurse enter next. The pompous and insensitive old gentleman cannot believe that Juliet refuses to comply with their arrangements. He upbraids her with being a "green-sickness carrion," a "baggage," and a "tallow face," and warns her to "fettle" her "fine joints 'gainst Thursday next," or he will drag her "on a hurdle thither."

Madam, if you could find out but a man
To bear a poison, I would temper it;   98
That Romeo should, upon receipt thereof,
Soon sleep in quiet. O, how my heart abhors
To hear him named and cannot come to him,
To wreak the love I bore my cousin   102
Upon his body that hath slaughtered him!
  Lady. Find thou the means, and I'll find such a man.
But now I'll tell thee joyful tidings, girl.
  Juliet. And joy comes well in such a needy time.
What are they, beseech your ladyship?
  Lady. Well, well, thou hast a careful father, child; 108
One who, to put thee from thy heaviness,
Hath sorted out a sudden day of joy   110
That thou expects not nor I looked not for.
  Juliet. Madam, in happy time! What day is that? 112
  Lady. Marry, my child, early next Thursday morn
The gallant, young, and noble gentleman,
The County Paris, at Saint Peter's Church,
Shall happily make thee there a joyful bride.
  Juliet. Now by Saint Peter's Church, and Peter, too,
He shall not make me there a joyful bride!
I wonder at this haste, that I must wed
Ere he that should be husband comes to woo.
I pray you tell my lord and father, madam,
I will not marry yet; and when I do, I swear
It shall be Romeo, whom you know I hate,
Rather than Paris. These are news indeed! 124
  Lady. Here comes your father. Tell him so yourself,
And see how he will take it at your hands. 126

Enter CAPULET *and* Nurse.

  Capulet. When the sun sets the earth doth drizzle
    dew,
But for the sunset of my brother's son
It rains downright.
How now? a conduit, girl? What, still in tears? 130
Evermore show'ring? In one little body
Thou counterfeit'st a bark, a sea, a wind:
For still thy eyes, which I may call the sea,
Do ebb and flow with tears; the bark thy body is,
Sailing in this salt flood; the winds, thy sighs,
Who, raging with thy tears and they with them,
Without a sudden calm will overset
Thy tempest-tossed body. How now, wife?
Have you delivered to her our decree?
  Lady. Ay, sir; but she will none, she gives you
    thanks.
I would the fool were married to her grave!
  Capulet. Soft! take me with you, take me with you, 142
    wife.
How? Will she none? Doth she not give us thanks?
Is she not proud? Doth she not count her blest, 144
Unworthy as she is, that we have wrought 145
So worthy a gentleman to be her bride?
  Juliet. Not proud you have, but thankful that you 147
    have.
Proud can I never be of what I hate,
But thankful even for hate that is meant love. 149
  Capulet. How, how, how, how, chopped-logic? 150
    What is this?

98. "temper": mix.

102. "wreak": pay.

108. "careful": one who cares for you.

110. "sorted out a sudden day": arranged an unexpected day (as in the next line).

112. "in happy time": for heaven's sake (expresses impatience).

124. "These are news": said sarcastically, referring to the "joyful tidings."

126. "at your hands": from you yourself (from your own lips).

130. "conduit": fountain.

142. "Soft! Take me with you": don't go so quickly; slow down so that I may understand you.

144. "proud": of such a marriage. "her": herself.

145. "wrought": arranged for.

147. "thankful": in so far as you have done it out of love for me.

149. "meant": meant for, or as.

150. "chop-logic": one who bandies logic; one who exchanges trivial points of logic.

ROMEO AND JULIET

ACT III SCENE V

Lady Capulet has the good taste, temporarily, to side with her daughter, but the old lord is adamant, and later threatens to disinherit and disown her if she continues to disobey him. Lady Capulet shortly withdraws her support from Juliet and leaves. Lord Capulet has already gone out.

'Proud'—and 'I thank you'—and 'I thank you not'—
And yet 'not proud'? Mistress minion you,   152
Thank me no thankings, nor proud me no prouds,   153
But fettle your fine joints 'gainst Thursday next   154
To go with Paris to Saint Peter's Church,
Or I will drag thee on a hurdle thither.   156
Out, you green-sickness carrion! out, you baggage!   157
You tallow-face!
    Lady.   Fie, fie! what, are you mad?   158
    Juliet. Good father, I beseech you on my knees,
Hear me with patience but to speak a word.
    Capulet. Hang thee, young baggage! disobedient
      wretch!
I tell thee what—get thee to church a Thursday
Or never after look me in the face.
Speak not, reply not, do not answer me!
My fingers itch. Wife, we scarce thought us blest   165
That God had lent us but this only child;
But now I see this one is one too much,
And that we have a curse in having her.
Out on her, hilding!   169
    Nurse.   God in heaven bless her!
You are to blame, my lord, to rate her so.   170
    Capulet. And why, my Lady Wisdom? Hold your
      tongue,
Good Prudence. Smatter with your gossips, go!   172
    Nurse. I speak no treason.
    Capulet.   O, God-i-god-en!   173
    Nurse. May not one speak?
    Capulet.   Peace, you mumbling fool!
Utter your gravity o'er a gossip's bowl,
For here we need it not.
    Lady.   You are too hot.   176
    Capulet. God's bread! it makes me mad.   177
Day, night; hour, tide, time; work, play;   178
Alone, in company; still my care hath been
To have her matched; and having now provided
A gentleman of noble parentage,
Of fair demesnes, youthful, and nobly trained,
Stuffed, as they say, with honorable parts,
Proportioned as one's thought would wish a man—
And then to have a wretched puling fool,   185
A whining mammet, in her fortune's tender,   186
To answer 'I'll not wed, I cannot love;
I am too young, I pray you pardon me'!
But, an you will not wed, I'll pardon you!   189
Graze where you will, you shall not house with me.
Look to't, think on't; I do not use to jest.   191
Thursday is near; lay hand on heart, advise:
An you be mine, I'll give you to my friend;
An you be not, hang, beg, starve, die in the streets,
For, by my soul, I'll ne'er acknowledge thee,
Nor what is mine shall never do thee good.
Trust to't. Bethink you. I'll not be forsworn.   197
                     [*Exit.*

    Juliet. Is there no pity in the clouds
That sees into the bottom of my grief?
O sweet my mother, cast me not away!
Delay this marriage for a month, a week;
Or if you do not, make the bridal bed

152. "minion": hussy, as employed here (ironic form of 'darling').

153. "Thank . . . prouds": do not argue with me. A common method of rebuff in Shakespeare's time.

154. "fettle": make ready.

156. "hurdle": a wooden framework in which prisoners were taken to punishment.

157. "carrion": no better than dead flesh. "baggage": hussy or minx.

158. "are you mad?": Lady Capulet may be joining in the attack on Juliet or (in view of her next speech) she may think that her husband is going too far.

165. "itch": to hit you.

169. "hilding": good-for-nothing fellow.

170. "rate": scold.

172. "Smatter": onomatopoetic word for gossip (parallel to chatter).

173. "God-i-god-en": God give you good evening—used here to dismiss the Nurse abruptly.

176. "hot": hot-tempered.

177. "God's bread": in the Sacrament.

178. "tide": time.

185. "puling": "whining."

186. "mammet": puppet or doll. "in her fortune's tender": when a good chance (of marriage) is offered her.

189. "pardon you": give you back your pardon (sarcastic).

191. "do not use": am not in the habit of.

197. "Trust to't": I mean it, you can rely on what I say. "forsworn": made to break my word to Paris.

Juliet, left alone with her nurse, is free to talk without double-entendre; the nurse gives her poor advice—now that Romeo is in exile, why not marry Paris? Juliet realizes how insubstantial and fickle the nurse is, and reverts to irony in the "Amen."

In the final soliloquy, beginning "Ancient damnation!" Juliet vows never to trust her nurse again: "Go, counsellor;/ Thou and my bosom henceforth shall be twain." She will make up her own mind, after seeking the "remedy" of Friar Laurence. She threatens to kill herself—"if all else fail."

The dramatic purposes achieved by this scene are:

1. It introduces a fresh complication for Juliet.

2. It develops the weak and selfish characters of Lord and Lady Capulet.

3. Juliet's sustained (later renewed) use of dramatic irony heightens interest.

4. It prepares us for the further plans of the following act.

In that dim monument where Tybalt lies.
Lady. Talk not to me, for I'll not speak a word.   204
Do as thou wilt, for I have done with thee.   [*Exit.*
Juliet. O God!—O nurse, how shall this be prevented?
My husband is on earth, my faith in heaven.   207
How shall that faith return again to earth
Unless that husband send it me from heaven
By leaving earth? Comfort me, counsel me.
Alack, alack, that heaven should practise stratagems   211
Upon so soft a subject as myself!
What say'st thou? Hast thou not a word of joy?
Some comfort, nurse.
  Nurse.   Faith, here it is.
Romeo is banished; and all the world to nothing   215
That he dares ne'er come back to challenge you;   216
Or if he do, it needs must be by stealth.
Then, since the case so stands as now it doth,
I think it best you married with the County.
O, he's a lovely gentleman!
Romeo's a dishclout to him. An eagle, madam,   221
Hath not so green, so quick, so fair an eye   222
As Paris hath. Beshrew my very heart,
I think you are happy in this second match,
For it excels your first; or if it did not,
Your first is dead—or 'twere as good he were
As living here and you no use of him.   227
  Juliet. Speak'st thou from thy heart?
  Nurse. And from my soul too; else beshrew them both.
  Juliet. Amen!   230
  Nurse. What?
  Juliet. Well, thou hast comforted me marvellous much.
Go in; and tell my lady I am gone,
Having displeased my father, to Laurence' cell,
To make confession and to be absolved.
  Nurse. Marry, I will; and this is wisely done. [*Exit.*
  Juliet. Ancient damnation! O most wicked fiend!   237
Is it more sin to wish me thus forsworn,   238
Or to dispraise my lord with that same tongue
Which she hath praised him with above compare
So many thousand times? Go, counsellor!
Thou and my bosom henceforth shall be twain.   242
I'll to the friar to know his remedy.
If all else fail, myself have power to die.   [*Exit.*

---

204. "I'll not speak a word": in your favor to your father.

207. "my faith": all I believe in. The general idea is very simple—there is no solution so long as Romeo remains alive.

211. "practise strategems": set cruel tricks.

215. "all the world to nothing": statement of odds.

216. "challenge": claim.

221. "dishclout": cloth for washing dishes.

222. "green": green eyes were much admired in Southern Europe.

227. "here": on earth.

230. "Amen!": Juliet confirms the Nurse's curse on her heart and soul, "beshrew them both."

237. "Ancient damnation": the old devil!

238. "forsworn": having broken my marriage vows.

242. "Thou . . . twain": I shall not come to you for counsel any more, we two must go our separate ways.

ACT IV SCENE I

At Friar Laurence's cell on Tuesday morning Count Paris tells the friar that he and Juliet are to be married on the following Thursday. The shortness of time appals the holy man, who realizes that some desperate action must be taken immediately to prevent a bigamous marriage, or worse.

Juliet enters to make her confession and, after an initial display of spirit, fatalistically proclaims "what must be shall be." This is a personal expression of resignation on the human level, but this sentiment also gives expression to the tragic doctrine of inevitability which runs through this drama, as it did through the tragic Greek dramas, lending coherence, 'significant form' and directed impetus to the play.

Friar Laurence entreats, "the time alone," and Paris leaves; in the confessional, Juliet breaks into tears, and laments the hopelessness of her position. Friar Laurence tells her he realizes what her problems are, but is powerless to solve them, whereupon she draws a knife and threatens to stab herself. Friar Laurence thinks of "a kind of hope,/Which craves as desperate an execution/As that is desperate which we would prevent." If Juliet is prepared to face actual death rather than marry Paris, she will probably be able to face simulated death as he will arrange it. Juliet is prepared to do this in order "to live an unstained wife" to her sweet love.

ACT FOUR, scene one.

(VERONA. FRIAR LAURENCE'S CELL)

Enter FRIAR LAURENCE *and* COUNTY PARIS.

Friar. On Thursday, sir? The time is very short.
Paris. My father Capulet will have it so,
And I am nothing slow to slack his haste.   3
Friar. You say you do not know the lady's mind.
Uneven is the course; I like it not.
Paris. Immoderately she weeps for Tybalt's death,
And therefore have I little talked of love;
For Venus smiles not in a house of tears.
Now, sir, her father counts it dangerous
That she do give her sorrow so much sway,
And in his wisdom hastes our marriage
To stop the inundation of her tears,
Which, too much minded by herself alone,   13
May be put from her by society.   14
Now do you know the reason of this haste.
Friar. [*aside*] I would I knew not why it should be   16
    slowed.—
Look, sir, here comes the lady toward my cell.

Enter JULIET.

Paris. Happily met, my lady and my wife!
Juliet. That may be, sir, when I may be a wife.
Paris. That 'may be' must be, love, on Thursday   20
    next.
Juliet. What must be shall be.
Friar.   That's a certain text.   21
Paris. Come you to make confession to this father?
Juliet. To answer that, I should confess to you.
Paris. Do not deny to him that you love me.
Juliet. I will confess to you that I love him.
Paris. So will ye, I am sure, that you love me.
Juliet. If I do so, it will be of more price,
Being spoke behind your back, than to your face.
Paris. Poor soul, thy face is much abused with tears.
Juliet. The tears have got small victory by that,
For it was bad enough before their spite.
Paris. Thou wrong'st it more than tears with that   32
    report.
Juliet. That is no slander, sir, which is a truth;
And what I spake, I spake it to my face.   34
Paris. Thy face is mine, and thou hast sland'red it.
Juliet. It may be so, for it is not mine own.   36
Are you at leisure, holy father, now,   37
Or shall I come to you at evening mass?
Friar. My leisure serves me, pensive daughter, now.
My lord, we must entreat the time alone.   40
Paris. God shield I should disturb devotion!   41
Juliet, on Thursday early will I rouse ye.
Till then, adieu, and keep this holy kiss.   [*Exit.*
Juliet. O, shut the door! and when thou hast
    done so,
Come weep with me—past hope, past cure, past help!
Friar. Ah, Juliet, I already know thy grief;
It strains me past the compass of my wits.

---

3. "slow to slack his haste": slow enough to delay his hurry.

13. "Which, too much minded by herself alone": she gives too much attention to her grief when she is by herself.

14. "society": the company of another.

16. "I would I knew not why . . .": I would prefer not to have such good reasons for the delay.

20. "That 'may be' must be": i.e., you must be mine.

21. "certain text": true saying.

32. "Thou": notice that when Paris starts to speak in tender fashion to Juliet he addresses her as "thou."

34. "And what I spake, I spake it to my face": not slanderously because openly.

36. "It is not mine own": her hidden meaning is that it is Romeo's.

37-38. "Are you . . . mass?": a polite hint to Paris that she wishes to be alone with the Friar.

40. "entreat the time alone": pray to be left alone for the time being.

41. "shield": forbid.

ROMEO AND JULIET

ACT IV SCENE I

This is Friar Laurence's plan to avoid Juliet's marrying Count Paris: on Wednesday evening she is to send her nurse out of the room, and, on climbing into bed, she will drink the distilled liquor from the vial provided by the friar. This liquor will put Juliet into a state of trance, and make her appear lifeless as a corpse. She will remain in the state of trance for forty-two hours, during which time her parents will have her "borne to that same ancient vault," where all the kindred of the Capulets lie."

In the meantime, Friar Laurence will inform Romeo of what has taken place, and call him back to Verona. He and Romeo will be present when Juliet comes out of the trance, and the friar will enable Romeo to bear Juliet "hence to Mantua."

I hear thou must, and nothing may prorogue it, 48
On Thursday next be married to this County.
   Juliet. Tell me not, friar, that thou hearest of this,
Unless thou tell me how I may prevent it.
If in thy wisdom thou canst give no help,
Do thou but call my resolution wise 53
And with this knife I'll help it presently. 54
God joined my heart and Romeo's, thou our hands;
And ere this hand, by thee to Romeo's sealed,
Shall be the label to another deed, 57
Or my true heart with treacherous revolt
Turn to another, this shall slay them both. 59
Therefore, out of thy long-experienced time,
Give me some present counsel; or, behold,
'Twixt my extremes and me this bloody knife 62
Shall play the umpire, arbitrating that 63
Which the commission of thy years and art
Could to no issue of true honor bring.
Be not so long to speak. I long to die
If what thou speak'st speak not of remedy.
   Friar. Hold, daughter. I do spy a kind of hope, 68
Which craves as desperate an execution 69
As that is desperate which we would prevent.
If, rather than to marry County Paris,
Thou hast the strength of will to slay thyself,
Then is it likely thou wilt undertake 73
A thing like death to chide away this shame, 74
That cop'st with death himself to scape from it; 75
And, if thou darest, I'll give thee remedy.
   Juliet. O, bid me leap, rather than marry Paris,
From off the battlements of any tower, 78
Or walk in thievish ways, or bid me lurk 79
Where serpents are; chain me with roaring bears,
Or hide me nightly in a charnel house,
O'ercovered quite with dead men's rattling bones,
With reeky shanks and yellow chapless skulls; 83
Or bid me go into a new-made grave
And hide me with a dead man in his shroud—
Things that, to hear them told, have made me
     tremble—
And I will do it without fear or doubt,
To live an unstained wife to my sweet love.
   Friar. Hold, then. Go home, be merry, give consent
To marry Paris. Wednesday is to-morrow.
To-morrow night look that thou lie alone; 91
Let not the nurse lie with thee in thy chamber.
Take thou this vial, being then in bed,
And this distilling liquor drink thou off;
When presently through all thy veins shall run
A cold and drowsy humor; for no pulse 96
Shall keep his native progress, but surcease; 97
No warmth, no breath, shall testify thou livest;
The roses in thy lips and cheeks shall fade
To wanny ashes, thy eyes' windows fall 100
Like death when he shuts up the day of life;
Each part, deprived of supple government, 102
Shall, stiff and stark and cold, appear like death; 103
And in this borrowed likeness of shrunk death
Thou shalt continue two-and-forty hours, 105
And then awake as from a pleasant sleep.

48. "prorogue": put off.

53. "resolution": i.e., to commit suicide.

54. "help it": i.e., "help my resolution," perhaps "further your wise advice." "presently": in the present, now.

57. "be the label to": seal. "deed": Euphemism.

59. "both": i.e., heart and hand.

62. "extremes": desperate position.

63. "play the umpire": i.e., decide between them.

63-65. "arbitrating . . . bring": deciding that which the authority of your years and knowledge could not honorably settle.

68. "Hold": here notice that the Friar's next two speeches after this one also begin with this word.

69. "as desperate an execution": as much desperation in putting (the plan) into effect.

73. "is it": it is.

74. "chide away": drive away.

75. "that cop'st with": a thing that has to do with . . . producing a state like death.

78. "any": i.e., however tall.

79. "thievish": i.e., where thieves abound.

83. "reeky shanks": smelly legs (between knee and ankle). "chapless": fleshless, lit. jawless.

91. "look": see. "lie": sleep.

96. "cold and drowsy humor": moisture carrying cold and sleeplessness.

97. "native": own. "surcease": cease.

100. "eyes' windows": eyelids (shutters).

102. "supple government": control that keeps limbs supple.

103. "stark": rigid, "stiff." "appear like death": no such drug is known to medicine or science.

105. "two-and-forty hours": actually the period of Juliet's "sleep" did not tally with the Friar's estimate.

ROMEO AND JULIET

ACT IV SCENE I

The dramatic purposes of this scene are:

1. To introduce the friar's remedy.

2. To heighten interest in the uniqueness of the plan, involving a romantic distilled liquor in a vial prepared by Friar Laurence, employing his knowledge of herbs (refer back to his long speech in Act II, Scene III).

3. It adumbrates the catastrophe in the Capulet's vault at the end of the tragedy.

Now, when the bridegroom in the morning comes
To rouse thee from thy bed, there art thou dead.
Then, as the manner of our country is,   109
In thy best robes uncovered on the bier   110
Thou shalt be borne to that same ancient vault
Where all the kindred of the Capulets lie.
In the mean time, against thou shalt awake,   113
Shall Romeo by my letters know our drift;   114
And hither shall he come; and he and I
Will watch thy waking, and that very night
Shall Romeo bear thee hence to Mantua.
And this shall free thee from this present shame,
If no inconstant toy nor womanish fear   119
Abate thy valor in the acting it.
   Juliet. Give me, give me! O, tell not me of fear!
   Friar. Hold! Get you gone, be strong and prosperous
In this resolve. I'll send a friar with speed
To Mantua, with my letters to thy lord.
   Juliet. Love give me strength! and strength shall 125
   help afford.
Farewell, dear father.   [*Exit with* Friar.

109. "as the manner of our country is": stated because this was an Italian, not an English, custom.

110. "uncovered on the bier": not in a coffin.

113. "against thou shalt awake": in readiness for thy awakening.

114. "drift": what we are driving at.

119. "inconstant toy": whimsical freak.

125. "help": i.e., the "remedy."

Scene two.

(THE SAME. HALL IN CAPULET'S HOUSE.)

Enter FATHER CAPULET, Mother, Nurse, *and*
Servingmen, *two or three.*

   Capulet. So many guests invite as here are writ.
                    [*Exit a* Servingman.
Sirrah, go hire me twenty cunning cooks.   2
   Servingman. You shall have none ill, sir; for I'll
try if they can lick their fingers.
   Capulet. How canst thou try them so?
   Servingman. Marry, sir, 'tis an ill cook that cannot
lick his own fingers. Therefore he that cannot lick   7
his fingers goes not with me.
   Capulet. Go, begone.   [*Exit* Servingman.
We shall be much unfurnished for this time.   10
What, is my daughter gone to Friar Laurence?
   Nurse. Ay, forsooth.
   Capulet. Well, he may chance to do some good on
   her.
A peevish self-willed harlotry it is.   14

              Enter JULIET.

   Nurse. See where she comes from shrift with merry 15
   look.
   Capulet. How now, my headstrong? Where have
   you been gadding?
   Juliet. Where I have learnt me to repent the sin
Of disobedient opposition
To you and your behests, and am enjoined
By holy Laurence to fall prostrate here
To beg your pardon. Pardon, I beseech you!
Henceforward I am ever ruled by you.
   Capulet. Send for the County. Go tell him of this.
I'll have this knot knit up to-morrow morning.   25

2. "cunning": skillful.

7. "lick his own fingers": taste his own products.

10. "much unfurnished": not ready.

14. "peevish": irritable to perversity. "harlotry": wantonness.

15. "shrift": confession.

25. "this knot": the marriage tie.

ACT IV SCENE II

The arrangements for the imminent wedding feast preoccupy Lord and Lady Capulet, now that Juliet, acting according to Friar Laurence's secret instructions, has apparently consented to marry Count Paris. She finds it necessary to deceive her parents in the interests of a more urgent loyalty.

Lord Capulet is in high good humor, and, forgetting that he intended to limit the reception to half a dozen guests, orders the Second Servingman to go and hire twenty knowledgeable and skillful cooks.

ROMEO AND JULIET

ACT IV SCENE II

Juliet, the epitome of "a peevish self-willed harlotry" to Capulet, enters, and reconciles herself to her father after begging his pardon. Old Capulet is so overjoyed by this new-found submissiveness that he orders the wedding advanced by a day, to Wednesday. He gives the credit for Juliet's change of attitude to "this reverend holy friar," Laurence. We perceive the dramatic irony in this ascription. Even Lady Capulet objects that Wednesday is too early, but her objection is ignored. Juliet and the nurse go to the bedchamber, while Capulet decides to stay up all night to superintend the preparations for the wedding breakfast. His heart is "wondrous light,/since this same wayward girl is so reclaimed."

The dramatic purposes of this scene are:

(1) it announces the putting ahead of the day of the marriage, thereby upsetting Friar Laurence's timing.

(2) it shows Juliet's apparently changed attitude towards the wedding.

ACT IV SCENE III

On Tuesday night, at bedtime, the curtain goes up on Juliet's bedchamber. She asks her "gentle nurse" to leave her to herself tonight, for she needs to pray. Actually, we realize, she needs to take the distilled liquor at once, twenty-four hours before the time named by Friar Laurence, since the marriage date has been advanced to Wednesday morning—only a few hours away.

It is necessary to understand that Juliet has not been successful in communicating this change of plan to the friar; therefore, the friar has not notified Romeo. This lack of communication will have catastrophic consequences, as we shall soon perceive.

Juliet tells Lady Capulet, in strangely formal terms, that she has made all the preparations necessary for the morrow, and requests that she be left alone with her nurse. Fortunately (?) Lady Capulet agrees.

The nurse now leaves, as previously arranged by Juliet, soon after Lady Capulet leaves. Left alone, Juliet feels cold and desolate; she longs for human companionship, and is tempted to call back her mother or nurse, but re-

---

Juliet. I met the youthful lord at Laurence' cell
And gave him what becomed love I might,   26
Not stepping o'er the bounds of modesty.
   Capulet. Why, I am glad on't. This is well. Stand up.
This is as't should be. Let me see the County.
Ay, marry, go, I say, and fetch him hither.
Now, afore God, this reverend holy friar,
All our whole city is much bound to him.
   Juliet. Nurse, will you go with me into my closet   33
To help me sort such needful ornaments
As you think fit to furnish me to-morrow?   35
   Mother. No, not till Thursday. There is time
     enough.
   Capulet. Go, nurse, go with her. We'll to church
     tomorrow.   [*Exeunt* JULIET *and* Nurse.
   Mother. We shall be short in our provision.   38
'Tis now near night.
   Capulet.   Tush, I will stir about,   39
And all things shall be well, I warrant thee, wife.
Go thou to Juliet, help to deck up her.
I'll not to bed to-night; let me alone.   42
I'll play the housewife for this once. What, ho!
They are all forth; well, I will walk myself   44
To County Paris, to prepare up him
Against to-morrow. My heart is wondrous light,
Since this same wayward girl is so reclaimed.   47
           [*Exit with* Mother.

Scene three.

(THE SAME. JULIET'S CHAMBER)

Enter JULIET *and* Nurse.

Juliet. Ay, those attires are best; but, gentle   1
   nurse,
I pray thee leave me to myself to-night;
For I have need of many orisons   3
To move the heavens to smile upon my state,   4
Which, well thou knowest, is cross and full of sin.   5
             Enter Mother.
   Mother. What, are you busy, ho? Need you my
   help?
   Juliet. No, madam; we have culled such neces-   7
   saries
As are behoveful for our state to-morrow.   8
So please you, let me now be left alone,
And let the nurse this night sit up with you;
For I am sure you have your hands full all   11
In this so sudden business.
   Mother.   Good night.
Get thee to bed, and rest; for thou hast need.
        [*Exeunt* Mother *and* Nurse.
   Juliet. Farewell! God knows when we shall meet
   again.
I have a faint cold fear thrills through my veins
That almost freezes up the heat of life.
I'll call them back again to comfort me.
Nurse!—What should she do here?   18

---

26. "becomed": fitting.

33. "closet": room.

35. "furnish me": prepare me for.

38. "provision": all the arrangements for the wedding, not just food.

39. "stir about": get moving.

42. "let me alone": i.e., leave things to me.

44. "They": the servants.
"forth": i.e., out.

47. "reclaimed": another metaphor from falconry; to "reclaim" a hawk was to recall it, or entice it back.

1. "attires": dresses.

3. "orisons": prayers (Fr. oraisons).

4. "state": i.e., of heart and mind.

5. "cross": perverse, wayward.

7. "culled": picked out; gathered (Fr. cueillir, to pluck).

8. "behoveful": necessary.
"state": pomp.

11. "all": entirely.

18. "What should she do": i.e., what good would she be?

ROMEO AND JULIET

ACT IV SCENE III

strains herself. She takes the fateful vial, and is filled with misgiving—"What if this mixture do not work at all?" She puts aside a dagger for use in the event that the drug fails to produce the desired effect; she would prefer suicide to a bigamous marriage with Paris.

She wonders whether the vial contains deadly poison, instead of the promised sleeping potion. She feels the friar "hath still been tried a holy man," though. Suppose she does fall asleep, as planned, but wakes "before the time that Romeo" comes to "redeem" her? Will she not suffocate in that "ancient receptacle" where Tybalt's body "lies festering in his shroud" along with the bones of all her "buried ancestors"? The prospect terrifies her. Her imagination conjures up a loathsome picture, of which hateful smells mandrakes' shrieks would make her run mad. In her frenzy, or hysteria, Juliet envisages Tybalt's ghost seeking out Romeo, to revenge himself. Calling out to him to stay, she says "Romeo, I come," and consumes the potion, thereupon falling lengthwise onto her four-posted bed within the curtains.

This scene, then, achieves the following dramatic purposes:

1. It records the drinking of the contents of the vial.

2. It stresses imaginatively the ghastly horror of the tomb—horror which is outdone only by the grisly actuality soon to be revealed.

3. It contrasts with the popular confusion of most of the previous scenes.

ACT IV SCENE IV

Six hours before the time set for the wedding of Juliet and Paris, Lord Capulet and the others are fussing over the details of the forthcoming breakfast, and talking of such trivialities as keys, spices, dates, quince and baked meat pies. The audience knows that Juliet lies in the adjoining room, either drugged or dead. This knowledge heightens the irony in a truly dramatic manner. Capulet's only anxiety is that the musicians of the County (Paris) will arrive before his servants are ready for the guests. Shakespeare presents this scene of bustling confusion over trivialities to occupy the time between the last scene and the next, and to provide comic relief.

My dismal scene I needs must act alone.   19
Come, vial.
What if this mixture do not work at all?
Shall I be married then to-morrow morning?
No, no! This shall forbid it. Lie thou there.
                [*Lays down a dagger.*
What if it be a poison which the friar
Subtly hath minist'red to have me dead,   25
Lest in this marriage he should be dishonored
Because he married me before to Romeo?
I fear it is; and yet methinks it should not,   28
For he hath still been tried a holy man.   29
How if, when I am laid into the tomb,
I wake before the time that Romeo
Come to redeem me? There's a fearful point!
Shall I not then be stifled in the vault,
To whose foul mouth no healthsome air breathes in,
And there die strangled ere my Romeo comes?   35
Or, if I live, is it not very like
The horrible conceit of death and night,   37
Together with the terror of the place—
As in a vault, an ancient receptacle   39
Where for this many hundred years the bones
Of all my buried ancestors are packed;
Where bloody Tybalt, yet but green in earth,   42
Lies fest'ring in his shroud; where, as they say,   43
At some hours in the night spirits resort—
Alack, alack, is it not like that I,
So early waking—what with loathsome smells,
And shrieks like mandrakes torn out of the earth,   47
That living mortals, hearing them, run mad—
O, if I wake, shall I not be distraught,
Environed with all these hideous fears,
And madly play with my forefathers' joints,
And pluck the mangled Tybalt from his shroud,
And, in this rage, with some great kinsman's bone
As with a club dash out my desp'rate brains?
O, look! methinks I see my cousin's ghost   55
Seeking out Romeo, that did spit his body   56
Upon a rapier's point. Stay, Tybalt, stay!   57
Romeo, I come! this do I drink to thee.   58
    [*She falls upon her bed within the curtains.*

Scene four.

(The Same. Hall in Capulet's House)

Enter Lady *of the House and* Nurse.

Lady. Hold, take these keys and fetch more spices, nurse.
Nurse. They call for dates and quinces in the pastry.   2
        Enter old CAPULET.
Capulet. Come, stir, stir, stir! The second cock hath crowed,
The curfew bell hath rung, 'tis three o'clock.   4
Look to the baked meats, good Angelica;   5
Spare not for cost.
Nurse.   Go, you cot-quean, go,   6

---

19. "dismal": disastrous.

25. "minist'red": prepared, provided.

28. "should not": is not likely to (be a poison).

29. "tried": found by experience.

35. "strangled": suffocated.

37. "conceit": imaginings, nightmares.

39. "As": (being) as it is.

42. "green": fresh (freshly placed).

43. "fest'ring": rotting.

47. "mandrakes torn": the mandrakes' shrieks when they (the mandrakes) are torn. The mandrake has a forked root, in popular imagination supposed to resemble a man or a duck (man-drake), and as it was used as a sleep-giving drug a number of superstitions clung about it. One was that it shrieked if torn out of the ground and the person who had pulled it went mad at the sound.

55. "my cousin's": Tybalt.

56. "spit": i.e., transfix, pierce through, as meat for roasting before the fire was impaled on a spit.

57. "stay": stop, do not do it.

58. "this do I drink to thee": she takes the Friar's potion as if drinking to Romeo's health thinking, in her imagination, to go to him when he needs her.

2. "pastry": the place where pastry was made.

4. "curfew bell": the alarm to wake the servants.

5. "baked meats": meat pies.

6. "cot-quean": man that busies himself unduly with matters belonging to the housewife's province ('quean' or hussy, of the cottage).

66

Without intervening delay Scene V follows. The nurse comes into the bedchamber and approaches Juliet's four-poster to draw back the curtains. She sees her mistress lying fully dressed on her bed. Shaking her, she feels how cold and stiff Juliet is, breaks out into loud lamentations and summons help. Lady Capulet rushes in, closely followed by her husband; they accept the fact of her death, and show a concern for her supposed corpse that they rarely showed for her when living.

Get you to bed! Faith, you'll be sick to-morrow
For this night's watching.   8
    Capulet. No, not a whit. What, I have watched ere now
All night for lesser cause, and ne'er been sick.
    Lady. Ay, you have been a mouse-hunt in your time;   11
But I will watch you from such watching now.   12
                              [*Exit* Lady *and* Nurse.
    Capulet. A jealous hood, a jealous hood!   13
    Enter three or four Fellows *with spits and logs and baskets.*
                            Now, fellow,
What is there?
    First Fellow. Things for the cook, sir; but I know not what.
    Capulet. Make haste, make haste. [*Exit first* Fellow.] Sirrah, fetch drier logs.
Call Peter; he will show thee where they are.
    Second Fellow. I have a head, sir, that will find out logs
And never trouble Peter for the matter.
    Capulet. Mass, and well said; a merry whoreson, ha!   20
Thou shalt be loggerhead. [*Exit second* Fellow, *with the others.*] Good Father! 'tis day.   21
The Country will be here with music straight,   22
For so he said he would.   *Play music.*   23
          I hear him near.
Nurse! Wife! What, ho! What, nurse, I say!
               Enter Nurse.
Go waken Juliet; go and trim her up.
I'll go and chat with Paris. Hie, make haste,   26
Make haste! The bridegroom he is come already:
Make haste, I say.   [*Exit.*

8. "watching": keeping awake—as in "Watch and pray."

11. "mouse-hunt": one who runs after women.

12. "watch you from such watching now": prevent you from running after women now by keeping watch on you.

13. "a jealous hood": jealous.

20. "whoreson": fellow.

21. "loggerhead": blockhead.

22. "music straight": i.e., musicians straightway. In Old England bride and bridegroom did not meet at the church. It was the custom for the bridegroom to call early for the bride to take her to church—with music in well-to-day families.

23. "for . . . would": he said so to Juliet too (IV.i.42)—assuming that the wedding would be on Thursday.

26. "Hie": away.

Scene five.

(THE SAME. JULIET'S CHAMBER)

Nurse *goes to curtains.*

    Nurse. Mistress! what, mistress! Juliet! Fast, I warrant her, she.   1
Why, lamb! why, lady! Fie, you slug-abed.   2
Why, love, I say! madam! sweetheart! Why, bride!
What, not a word? You take your pennyworths now;   4
Sleep for a week; for the next night, I warrant,
The Country Paris hath set up his rest
That you shall rest but little. God forgive me!
Marry, and amen. How sound is she asleep!
I needs must wake her. Madam, madam, madam!
Ay, let the County take you in your bed;
He'll fright you up, i' faith. Will it not be?   11
              [*Draws aside the curtains.*
What, dressed, and in your clothes, and down again?
I must needs wake you. Lady! lady! lady!
Alas, alas! Help, help! my lady's dead!

1. "what": a loud call.
"Fast": fast asleep.

2. "slug-abed": lit. slug in a bed, i.e., lazy creature.

4. "pennyworths": small quantities (of sleep); pronounced 'pennorths.'

11. "will it not be?": i.e., will you not wake up?
"fright you up": scare you awake.

ROMEO AND JULIET

ACT IV SCENE V

Friar Laurence and Paris enter, with musicians—whose presence is suddenly strangely out of keeping in the "death" chamber. The only calm voice in the hysterical outbreak of grief that ensues is the friar's, pointing out the illogicality of mourning for Juliet "now heaven hath all."

O weraday that ever I was born! 15
Some aqua vitae, ho! My lord! my lady! 16

Enter Mother.

Mother. What noise is here?
Nurse.   O lamentable day!
Mother. What is the matter?
Nurse.   Look, look! O heavy day!
Mother. O me, O me! My child, my only life! 19
Revive, look up, or I will die with thee!
Help, help! Call help.

Enter Father.

Father. For shame, bring Juliet forth; her lord is
    come.
Nurse. She's dead, deceased; she's dead, alack the
    day!
Mother. Alack the day, she's dead, she's dead, she's
    dead!
Capulet. Ha! let me see her. Out alas! she's cold, 25
Her blood is settled, and her joints are stiff; 26
Life and these lips have long been separated.
Death lies on her like an untimely frost
Upon the sweetest flower of all the field.
Nurse. O lamentable day!
Mother.   O woeful time!
Capulet. Death, that hath ta'en her hence to make
    me wail,
Ties up my tongue and will not let me speak.

Enter FRIAR LAURENCE *and the* COUNTY PARIS, *with*
    Musicians.

Friar. Come, is the bride ready to go to church?
Capulet. Ready to go, but never to return.
O son, the night before thy wedding day
Hath Death lain with thy wife. There she lies,
Flower as she was, deflowered by him. 37
Death is my son-in-law, Death is my heir;
My daughter he hath wedded. I will die
And leave him all. Life, living, all is Death's. 40
Paris. Have I thought long to see this morning's 41
    face,
And doth it give me such a sight as this?
Mother. Accursed, unhappy, wretched, hateful day!
Most miserable hour that e'er time saw
In lasting labor of his pilgrimage! 45
But one, poor one, one poor and loving child,
But one thing to rejoice and solace in,
And cruel Death hath catched it from my sight.
Nurse. O woe! O woeful, woeful, woeful day!
Most lamentable day, most woeful day
That ever ever I did yet behold!
O day, O day, O day! O hateful day!
Never was seen so black a day as this.
O woeful day! O woeful day!
Paris. Beguiled, divorced, wronged, spited, slain!
Most detestable Death, by thee beguiled,
By cruel cruel thee quite overthrown.
O love! O life! not life, but love in death!
Capulet. Despised, distressed, hated, martyred, 59
    killed!
Uncomfortable time, why cam'st thou now 60
To murder, murder our solemnity?

15. "weraday": alas the day.
16. "aqua vitae": brandy, a favorite remedy.

19. "my only life": life itself to me.

25. "Out": intensified "alas!"
26. "settled": congealed.

37. "deflowered by": having surrendered her maidenhead to him.

40. "living": means of life, possessions.
41. "thought long to see this morning's face": looked forward to seeing for a long time.

45. "lasting": i.e., the long unending.

59. "Despised": i.e., by fate.
60. "Uncomfortable": with no comfort.

Capulet orders the "festival" turned into a "funeral," and "all things" changed "to the contrary." Friar Laurence tells everybody to prepare to follow "this fair corse" to her grave. He utters a pregnant warning:

The heavens do lower upon you for some ill;

Move them no more by crossing their high will.

This warning is in keeping with the impetus to catastrophe which has been gathering momentum with tragic inevitability in this drama so far.

The indifferent jesting of the musicians serves to relieve the gloom of the rest of the scene.

O child, O child! my soul, and not my child! 62
Dead art thou—alack, my child is dead,
And with my child my joys are buried!
  Friar. Peace, ho, for shame! Confusion's cure lives not 65
In these confusions. Heaven and yourself
Had part in this fair maid—now heaven hath all,
And all the better is it for the maid.
Your part in her you could not keep from death,
But heaven keeps his part in eternal life. 70
The most you sought was her promotion,
For 'twas your heaven she should be advanced; 72
And weep ye now, seeing she is advanced 73
Above the clouds, as high as heaven itself?
O, in this love, you love your child so ill
That you run mad, seeing that she is well. 76
She's not well married that lives married long,
But she's best married that dies married young.
Dry up your tears and stick your rosemary
On this fair corse, and, as the custom is,
In all her best array bear her to church;
For though fond nature bids us all lament, 82
Yet nature's tears are reason's merriment. 83
  Capulet. All things that we ordained festival
Turn from their office to black funeral—
Our instruments to melancholy bells, 86
Our wedding cheer to a sad burial feast;
Our solemn hymns to sullen dirges change;
Our bridal flowers serve for buried corse;
And all things change them to the contrary. 90
  Friar. Sir, go you in; and, madam, go with him;
And go, Sir Paris. Every one prepare
To follow this fair corse unto her grave.
The heavens do low'r upon you for some ill; 94
Move them no more by crossing their high will. 95
[*Exeunt casting rosemary on her and shutting the curtains.*

[*Manet the* Nurse *with Musicians.*
First Musician. Faith, we may put up our pipes and be gone. 96
  Nurse. Honest good fellows, ah, put up, put up!
For well you know this is a pitiful case. [*Exit.* 98
First Musician. Ay, by my troth, the case may be amended. 99

Enter PETER.

Peter. Musicians, O, musicians, 'Heart's ease,' 100
'Heart's ease'!
O, an you will have me live, play 'Heart's ease.'
  First Musician. Why 'Heart's ease'?
Peter. O, musicians, because my heart itself plays
'My heart is full of woe.' O, play me some merry dump to comfort me.
  First Musician. Not a dump we! 'Tis no time to play 106
now.
Peter. You will not then?
First Musician. No.
Peter. I will then give it you soundly. 109
First Musician. What will you give us?
  Peter. No money, on my faith, but the gleek. I will 111
give you the minstrel.

62. "not": i.e., not now.

65. "Confusion's": destruction. In the next line the word has more its modern sense.

70. "In eternal life": in the life she now enjoys.

72. "heaven": i.e., idea of what was best.

73. "advanced": i.e., in life.

76. "well": i.e., in heaven.

82. "fond nature": foolish natural feeling.

83. "reason's merriment": laugh-raising when considered from the viewpoint of reason.

86. "instruments": musical instruments.

90. "them": themselves.

94. "ill": i.e., evil deed that you have done.

95. "Move": anger.

96. "put up our pipes": pack up.

98. "pitiful case": sad state of affairs.

99. "case": musical instrument case.

100-4. "heart's ease": "my heart is full of woe": both popular English songs at the end of the sixteenth century. The second is the chorus of a ballad called "A Pleasant New Ballad of Two Lovers"; by Richard Edwards. It is quoted later in the scene.

106. "dump": tune (a sad one).

109. "give it you soundly": let you have it thoroughly. The pun on the word used to a musician is obvious.

111. "gleek": jest, mock.
"give you the minstrel": call you 'minstrel.'

Dramatically, the scene achieves two purposes:

1. The preparations for Juliet's entombment prepare the audience for the denouement, or tying of the tragic knot in Aristotelian terms.

2. It bridges the interval between this scene and the forthcoming fifth act with trivial bantering among Peter and the musicians, who plan to wait "for the mourners, and stay dinner."

ACT V SCENE 1

On stage is Romeo, in exile on a street of Mantua. He is unaccustomedly cheerful, and expects some good news from Verona. He has had a dream in which his lady came and found him dead, but breathed such life with kisses into his lips that he revived and became an emperor. Shakespeare knew how to invert the elements belonging to the structure of the dream as well as Sigmund Freud.

First Musician. Then will I give you the serving- 113
creature.
Peter. Then will I lay the serving-creature's dagger
on your pate. I will carry no crotchets. I'll re you, 115
I'll fa you. Do you note me?
First Musician. An you re us and fa us, you note us. 117
Second Musician. Pray you put up your dagger,
and put out your wit. 119
Peter. Then have at you with my wit! I will dry-beat 120
you with an iron wit, and put up my iron dagger.
Answer me like men.
 'When griping grief the heart doth wound,
  And doleful dumps the mind oppress,
  Then music with her silver sound'—
Why 'silver sound'? Why 'music with her silver
 sound'?
What say you, Simon Catling? 127
First Musician. Marry, sir, because silver hath a
 sweet sound.
Peter. Pretty! What say you, Hugh Rebeck? 129
Second Musician. I say 'silver sound' because musi-
cians sound for silver. 131
Peter. Pretty too! What say you, James Soundpost? 132
Third Musician. Faith, I know not what to say.
Peter. O, I cry you mercy! you are the singer. I will 134
say for you. It is 'music with her silver sound' be-
cause musicians have no gold for sounding. 136
'Then music with her silver sound 137
With speedy help doth lend redress.' [*Exit.*
First Musician. What a pestilent knave is this same!
Second Musician. Hang him, Jack! Come, we'll in 140
here, tarry for the mourners, and stay dinner.
         [*Exit with others.*

ACT FIVE, scene one.

(MANTUA. A STREET)

Enter ROMEO.

Romeo. If I may trust the flattering truth of sleep, 1
My dreams presage some joyful news at hand.
My bosom's lord sits lightly in his throne, 3
And all this day an unaccustomed spirit
Lifts me above the ground with cheerful thoughts.
I dreamt my lady came and found me dead 6
(Strange dream that gives a dead man leave to 7
 think!)
And breathed such life with kisses in my lips
That I revived and was an emperor. 9
Ah me! how sweet is love itself possessed, 10
When but love's shadows are so rich in joy! 11

Enter ROMEO's *Man* BALTHASAR, *booted.*

News from Verona! How now, Balthasar? 12
Dost thou not bring me letters from the friar? 13
How doth my lady? Is my father well?
How fares my Juliet? That I ask again,
For nothing can be ill if she be well.

113. "give you the serving-creature": call you a servant "Creature" adds a note of contempt. Notice that to call anyone a "minstrel" was as insulting as to call him a "serving-creature."

115. "carry": endure. "crotchets": whims.

117. "re .. fa": terms from the tonic sol-fa (system of musical tones).

119. "put out": extinguish.

120. "have at you": I challenge you. "dry-beat": refer to note to Act III, Scene I, line 78.

127. "Catling": catgut.

129. "Rebeck": A three-stringed fiddle.

131. "for silver": i.e., to be paid.

132. "Soundpost": the name of the piece of wood fixed near the bridge of a violin to keep the back and the belly apart.

134. "you are the singer": and therefore cannot "say." Peter is still playing with words. "cry you mercy": beg your pardon.

136. "sounding": i.e., the music they make.

137-8. "'Then music . . . redress'": he completes the stanza he started above.

140. "Jack": refer to Act II, Scene IV, line 140.

1. "trust the flattering truth of sleep": trust the pictures which we see in dreams, but which are seldom realized in life.

3. "bosom's lord": love. "his throne": the heart.

6. "I dreamt . . . dead": a reversal of the actual. Amongst all his happiness this gives a presentiment of evil without telling us just how things are going to happen.

7. "gives": permits.

9. "an emperor": lord of all.

10. "possessed": enjoyed.

11. "but love's shadows": merely dreams of love.

12. "How now": corresponding to our exclamation, "What now?"

13-15. "Dost . . . again": the way in which Romeo fires question after question at Balthasar without waiting for an answer is very natural: it shows the excitement of a lonely banished man on seeing someone with news. Notice that Romeo addresses his servant as "thou," but Balthasar his master as "you." See Glossary, Act I, Scene III, line 9.

ROMEO AND JULIET

ACT V SCENE I

Balthasar comes in, booted, from Verona, bringing the sad news that Juliet it dead. Romeo determines to defy the edict of banishment and return to his native city, with post-horses, "to-night." Balthasar is disturbed at Romeo's haste and appearance, and fears "some misadventure."

Romeo visits a poor Apothecary, or druggist, and purchases for forty gold ducats a small quantity of a deadly poison powder noted for its virulence and rapidity of operation. The Apothecary is reluctant to sell this poison, but his poverty consents to do so. The sale is illegal, and Romeo pays a fortune for it. The poison needs to be dissolved in water, and drunk. It will kill twenty men at once.

Man. Then she is well, and nothing can be ill. 17
Her body sleeps in Capel's monument, 18
And her immortal part with angels lives.
I saw her laid low in her kindred's vault
And presently took post to tell it you. 21
O, pardon me for bringing these ill news,
Since you did leave it for my office, sir. 23
Romeo. Is it e'en so? Then I defy you, stars! 24
Thou knowest my lodging. Get me ink and paper 25
And hire posthorses. I will hence to-night.
Man. I do beseech you, sir, have patience.
Your looks are pale and wild and do import 28
Some misadventure.
Romeo.　　　　Tush, thou art deceived.
Leave me and do the thing I bid thee do.
Hast thou no letters to me from the friar?
Man. No, my good lord.
Romeo.　　　No matter. Get thee gone
And hire those horses. I'll be with thee straight.
　　　　　　　　　　　　　　[Exit BALTHASAR.
Well, Juliet, I will lie with thee to-night. 34
Let's see for means. O mischief, thou art swift 35
To enter in the thoughts of desperate men!
I do remember an apothecary, 37
And hereabouts 'a dwells, which late I noted 38
In tatt'red weeds, with overwhelming brows, 39
Culling of simples. Meagre were his looks, 40
Sharp misery had worn him to the bones;
And in his needy shop a tortoise hung, 42
An alligator stuffed, and other skins 43
Of ill-shaped fishes; and about his shelves 44
A beggarly account of empty boxes, 45
Green earthen pots, bladders, and musty seeds, 46
Remnants of packthread, and old cakes of roses 47
Were thinly scattered, to make up a show.
Noting this penury, to myself I said,
'An if a man did need a poison now
Whose sale is present death in Mantua, 51
Here lives a caitiff wretch would sell it him.' 52
O, this same thought did but forerun my need, 53
And this same needy man must sell it me.
As I remember, this should be the house.
Being holiday, the beggar's shop is shut.
What, ho! apothecary!

Enter APOTHECARY.

Apothecary.　　　Who calls so loud?
Romeo. Come hither, man. I see that thou art poor.
Hold, there is forty ducats. Let me have
A dram of poison, such soon-speeding gear 60
As will disperse itself through all the veins
That the life-weary taker may fall dead,
And that the trunk may be discharged of breath 63
As violently as hasty powder fired
Doth hurry from the fatal cannon's womb. 65
Apothecary. Such mortal drugs I have; but Mantua's law
Is death to any he that utters them. 67
Romeo. Art thou so bare and full of wretchedness 68
And fearest to die? Famine is in thy cheeks,
Need and oppression starveth in thy eyes, 70

17. "well": Balthasar is trying to break the news gently, using the word to mean (for himself) "in peace."

18. "Capels": in Brooke's Romeus and Juliet Capel and Capulet are used indiscriminately.

21. "presently": at once.
"took post": started my journey, using post-horses.

23. "office": duty.

24. "stars": my fate.

25-26. "Get . . . to-night": notice the curt decisiveness of these comments.

28. "import": mean, signify.

34. "I will lie with thee to-night": as a corpse in a tomb.

35. "means": means to do it.

37. "I do remember an apothecary": Romeo has soon found his way about Mantua!

38. "which": whom.

39. "weeds": clothes.
"overwhelming': overhanging.

40. "of": the "of" is inserted because "culling" is a verbal noun.
"simples": medicinal herbs.
"meagre": thin (Fr. maigre).

42. "needy": in need, bare.

43. "alligator stuffed": the sign of an apothecary.

44. "ill-shaped fishes": fish of evil shape.

45. "beggarly account": very small number.

46. "bladders": to hold liquids.

47. "packthread": stout thread.
"cakes of roses": rose leaves pressed together (for their scent).

51. "present": at present (see line 21).

52. "caitiff": wretched (from its original meaning, captive).

53. "forerun": anticipate.

60. "soon-speeding gear": something to kill a man rapidly.

63. "trunk": body.

65. "fatal": death-dealing.

67. "he": person.
"utters": puts on sale.

68. "bare": half-starved.

70. "Need . . . eyes": it can be seen from your eyes that want and oppression are killing you.

ACT V SCENE I

The dramatic purposes of this scene are:

1. To give Romeo a relatively cheerful and optimistic outlook at the beginning of the scene, so that his hopes may be dashed and his courage turned to despair by contrast.

2. To illustrate (by omission) the miscarriage of the Friar's plans.

3. To show the immediate effect of Juliet's 'death' on Romeo, and thereby to prepare us for a catastrophe ahead.

ACT V SCENE II

Meanwhile, at Verona, Friar Laurence is met by Friar John, the messenger who had been sent to tell Romeo all the details of the vial-arrangement. Friar John was not able to reach Romeo owing to his having been put in quarantine owing to an outbreak of the plague. He hands Friar Laurence the letter, intended for Romeo, which he has been unable to deliver.

The Friar utters an exclamatory oxymoron—" unhappy fortune!"—and, in deadly haste, sends Friar John to fetch him an iron crowbar. Laurence plans to go alone to the Capulet vault (monument) since Juliet will be waking up within three hours. She will blame the friar for failing to inform Romeo, but he intends to look after her until a second letter has been sent to Romeo in Mantua.

He hurries off to the tomb, pitying the "poor living corse" (another oxymoron!) enclosed in a "dead man's tomb."

The dramatic purpose of this scene is to show how an accident of fate interfered with the successful execution of these well-laid plans.

Contempt and beggary hangs upon thy back: 71
The world is not thy friend, nor the world's law;
The world affords no law to make thee rich;   73
Then be not poor, but break it and take this.   74
   Apothecary. My poverty but not my will consents.
   Romeo. I pay thy poverty and not thy will.
   Apothecary. Put this in any liquid thing you will
And drink it off, and if you had the strength
Of twenty men, it would dispatch you straight.
   Romeo. There is thy gold—worse poison to men's souls,
Doing more murder in this loathsome world,
Than these poor compounds that thou mayst not sell.
I sell thee poison; thou hast sold me none.   83
Farewell. Buy food and get thyself in flesh.   84
Come, cordial and not poison, go with me   85
To Juliet's grave; for there must I use thee.
                       [*Exeunt.*

Scene two.

(VERONA. FRIAR LAURENCE'S CELL)

Enter FRIAR JOHN *to* FRIAR LAURENCE.

John. Holy Franciscan friar, brother, ho!

Enter FRIAR LAURENCE.

Laurence. This same should be the voice of Friar John.
Welcome from Mantua. What says Romeo?
Or, if his mind be writ, give me his letter.
   John. Going to find a barefoot brother out,   5
One of our order, to associate me   6
Here in this city visiting the sick,
And finding him, the searchers of the town,
Suspecting that we both were in a house
Where the infectious pestilence did reign,
Sealed up the doors, and would not let us forth,   11
So that my speed to Mantua there was stayed.   12
   Laurence. Who bare my letter, then, to Romeo?
   John. I could not send it—here it is again—
Nor get a messenger to bring it thee,
So fearful were they of infection.   16
   Laurence. Unhappy fortune! By my brotherhood,
The letter was not nice, but full of charge,   18
Of dear import; and the neglecting it   19
May do much danger. Friar John, go hence,
Get me an iron crow and bring it straight   21
Unto my cell.
   John.   Brother, I'll go and bring it thee.   [*Exit.*
   Laurence. Now must I to the monument alone.
Within this three hours will fair Juliet wake.
She will beshrew me much that Romeo   25
Hath had no notice of these accidents;   26
But I will write again to Mantua,
And keep her at my cell till Romeo come—
Poor living corse, closed in a dead man's tomb!
                       [*Exit.*

71. "Contempt": the cause of other men's contempt.

73. "affords": provides.

74. "it": the law.

83. "I sell . . . none": gold is a worse poison that this drug. (It has been proved so in this transaction).

84. "in flesh": better covered with flesh.

85. "cordial": drug with powers of revival (from Latin cor, heart).

5. "barefoot brother": the Franciscans were enjoined to walk barefoot, and friars usually travelled in pairs.

6. "associate": accompany.

11. "Sealed up": put the official seal on, indicating that no one was allowed to enter or leave the house. This was the sixteenth-century method of isolating people with the plague.

12. "stayed": delayed.

16. "they": the messengers.

18. "nice": trivial (too many unimportant details).
"charge": importance, weight.

19. "dear": great.

21. "crow": crowbar.

25. "beshrew": blame.

26. "accidents": events.

ACT V SCENE III

The setting is the Capulet monument, in the churchyard, and it is night. Paris and his page boy enter to place flowers on Juliet's tomb. The page boy is told to wait unseen behind a neighboring yew tree, to listen carefully, ear close to ground, and to whistle if anybody approaches.

Paris strews the flowers on Juliet's tomb, when suddenly the page whistles; he hides, and Romeo enters with Balthasar. Romeo goes up to the door of the tomb, seizes a mattock, and wrenches it open. He hands a letter addressed to his father to Balthasar, and, taking the flaming torch, descends alone into the "bed of death." His purpose is partly to see Juliet's face once more, and partly to take a precious ring from her dead finger. If anybody should dare to return to pry on him, Romeo threatens to tear him "joint by joint" and scatter the limbs over "this hungry churchyard..." Faced with such a threat, Balthasar leaves Romeo to his own devices, after pocketing a gold piece proffered by Romeo. Shortly afterwards Balthasar hides himself nearby, because he mistrusts Romeo's intentions, and fears his looks.

Romeo opens the tomb, but Paris recognizes him as "that banished haughty Montague" and fears that he intends to desecrate the tomb by some villainous and shameful act. He challenges Romeo, and they fight. His page-boy rushes away, fearfully, to summon the watch. Romeo succeeds in slaying Paris, and Romeo promises to lay his body with that of Juliet. Romeo then goes down, bearing Paris' noble body, and lays it next to Juliet. He observes that her frame is still unconquered by physical decay:

... beauty's ensign yet

Is crimson in thy lips and in thy cheeks,

And death's pale flag is not advanced there.

Scene three.

(THE SAME. A CHURCHYARD; IN IT A MONUMENT BELONGING TO THE CAPULETS)

Enter PARIS *and his* Page *with flowers and sweet water.*

Paris. Give me thy torch, boy. Hence, and stand
    aloof.   1
Yet put it out, for I would not be seen.
Under yond yew tree lay thee all along,
Holding thy ear close to the hollow ground.
So shall no foot upon the churchyard tread
(Being loose, uniform, with digging up of graves)
But thou shalt hear it. Whistle then to me,
As signal that thou hearest something approach.
Give me those flowers. Do as I bid thee, go.
   Page. (aside) I am almost afraid to stand alone   10
Here in the churchyard; yet I will adventure.
                        [*Retires.*
   Paris. Sweet flower, with flowers thy bridal bed I 12
    strew
(O woe! thy canopy is dust and stones)
Which with sweet water nightly I will dew;   14
Or, wanting that, with tears distilled by moans.
The obsequies that I for thee will keep   16
Nightly shall be to strew thy grave and weep.
                       [*Whistle* Boy.
The boy gives warning something doth approach.
What cursed foot wanders this way to-night
To cross my obsequies and true love's rite?   20
What, with a torch? Muffle me, night, awhile.
                       [*Retires.*
Enter ROMEO, *and* BALTHASAR *with a torch, a mattock,*
and a crow of iron.

   Romeo. Give me that mattock and the wrenching 22
    iron.
Hold, take this letter. Early in the morning
See thou deliver it to my lord and father.
Give me the light. Upon thy life I charge thee,
Whate'er thou hearest or seest, stand all aloof
And do not interrupt me in my course.
Why I descend into this bed of death   28
Is partly to behold my lady's face,
But chiefly to take thence from her dead finger
A precious ring—a ring that I must use
In dear employment. Therefore hence, be gone.   32
But if thou, jealous, dost return to pry
In what I farther shall intend to do,
By heaven, I will tear thee joint by joint
And strew this hungry churchyard with thy limbs.
The time and my intents are savage-wild,   37
More fierce and more inexorable far
Than empty tigers or the roaring sea.   39
   Balthasar. I will be gone, sir, and not trouble you.
   Romeo. So shalt thou show me friendship. Take
    thou that.   41
Live, and be prosperous; and farewell, good fellow.

1. "aloof": apart.

2. "Yet": further—an order amending his first.

3. "all along": flat.

10. "stand": be, remain.

12. "Sweet flower": refers to Juliet.

14. "sweet": perfumed.

16. "obsequies": rites of burial. "keep": observe.

20. "cross": interfere with.

22. "mattock": like a pickaxe, only with an arched blade at one side.

28. "Why": the reason why.

32. "dear": important.

33. "jealous": suspicious.

37. "The time": Romeo probably means the time after Juliet's death, but perhaps simply the dead of night.

39. "empty": and therefore savage.

41. "that": a money present.

ROMEO AND JULIET

ACT V SCENE III

He perceives Tybalt lying there in a bloody sheet, and bitterly regrets that he can do nothing more for him than end his own wretched existence. This Romeo now does by drinking the Apothecary's quick poison. "Quick" also means living—and it is significant of the grotesque and melodramatic character of this gruesome scene that Romeo should die with a pun on his lips. A true Elizabethan!

Balthasar. [*aside*] For all this same, I'll hide me hereabout. 43

His looks I fear, and his intents I doubt.　　　　[*Retires.* 44

Romeo. Thou detestable maw, thou womb of death,

Gorged with the dearest morsel of the earth,

Thus I enforce thy rotten jaws to open,

And in despite I'll cram thee with more food. 48

　　　　[ROMEO *opens the tomb.*

Paris. This is that banished haughty Montague

That murd'red my love's cousin—with which grief

It is supposed the fair creature died—

And here is come to do some villainous shame

To the dead bodies. I will apprehend him.

Stop thy unhallowed toil, vile Montague!

Can vengeance be pursued further than death? 55

Condemned villain, I do apprehend thee.

Obey, and go with me; for thou must die.

Romeo. I must indeed; and therefore came I hither.

Good gentle youth, tempt not a desp'rate man.

Fly hence and leave me. Think upon these gone; 60

Let them affright thee. I beseech thee, youth, 61

Put not another sin upon my head 62

By urging me to fury. O, be gone!

By heaven, I love thee better than myself,

For I come hither armed against myself. 65

Stay not, be gone. Live, and hereafter say

A madman's mercy bid thee run away.

Paris. I do defy thy conjuration 68

And apprehend thee for a felon here.

Romeo. Wilt thou provoke me? Then have at thee, boy!　　　　[*They fight.*

Page. O Lord, they fight! I will go call the watch. 71

　　　　[*Exit.* PARIS *falls.*

Paris. O, I am slain! If thou be merciful,

Open the tomb, lay me with Juliet.　　　　[*Dies.*

Romeo. In faith, I will. Let me peruse this face. 74

Mercutio's kinsman, noble County Paris! 75

What said my man when my betossed soul

Did not attend him as we rode? I think 77

He told me Paris should have married Juliet.

Said he not so? or did I dream it so?

Or am I mad, hearing him talk of Juliet,

To think it was so? O, give me thy hand,

One writ with me in sour misfortune's book!

I'll bury thee in a triumphant grave. 83

A grave? O, no, a lanthorn, slaught'red youth, 84

For here lies Juliet, and her beauty makes

This vault a feasting presence full of light. 86

Death, lie thou there, by a dead man interred. 87

　　　　[*Lays him in the tomb.*

How oft when men are at the point of death

Have they been merry! which their keepers call 89

A lightning before death. O, how may I 90

Call this a lightning? O my love! my wife!

Death, that hath sucked the honey of thy breath, 92

Hath had no power yet upon thy beauty.

Thou art not conquered. Beauty's ensign yet 94

Is crimson in thy lips and in thy cheeks,

And death's pale flag is not advanced there.

Tybalt, liest thou there in thy bloody sheet? 97

43. "For all this same": Notwithstanding all this.

44. "His looks I fear": Balthasar fears what Romeo may do to himself.

48. "in despite": against your wish.

55. "Can vengeance . . . death?" Paris thinks that Romeo has come to desecrate the Capulet tomb, in particular the body of Tybalt.

60. "these gone": the surrounding dead.

61. "affright thee": the implication is, "And prevent your hindering me."

62. "another sin": killing you.

65. "armed against myself": with the poison (suicidal).

68. "conjuration": sworn warnings.

71. "watch": the Elizabethan police.

74. "peruse": look closely at.

75. "Mercutio's kinsman": both Mercutio and Paris were kinsmen of the Prince.

77. "attend him": pay attention to what he was saying.

83. "triumphant": splendid.

84. "lanthorn": lantern.

86. "presence": royal apartment.

87. "death": Paris' body. "a dead man": Romeo's body.

89. "keepers": attendants. Romeo is not necessarily thinking of men at the point of death in prison.

90. "lightning": lightening (of the spirits).

92. "honey": sweetness.

94. "ensign": flag standard.

97. "sheet": winding sheet.

At the other end of the churchyard, Friar Laurence stumbles toward the tomb, also equipped with lantern, crowbar and spade. He meets Balthasar, who explains that the light burning in the open tomb belongs to his master, Romeo. From now on the course of events is something of an anti-climax.

Friar Laurence is alarmed to learn that Romeo has been down there "full half an hour," and when Balthasar refuses to accompany him, decides to venture down alone. He discovers Paris' blood stains, then the bodies of Romeo and Paris, and as he approaches Juliet's vault, she awakes. She sees the Friar, and, scared by "some noise" within, he blurts out the dreadful facts, and bids her come away from "that nest of death, contagion, and unnatural sleep."

O, what more favor can I do to thee
Than with that hand that cut thy youth in twain
To sunder his that was thine enemy?
Forgive me, cousin! Ah, dear Juliet,   101
Why art thou yet so fair? Shall I believe
That unsubstantial Death is amorous,   103
And that the lean abhorred monster keeps
Thee here in dark to be his paramour?
For fear of that I still will stay with thee
And never from this pallet of dim night
Depart again. Here, here will I remain
With worms that are thy chambermaids. O, here
Will I set up my everlasting rest
And shake the yoke of inauspicious stars   111
From this world-wearied flesh. Eyes, look your last!
Arms, take your last embrace! and lips, O you
The doors of breath, seal with a righteous kiss
A dateless bargain to engrossing death!   115
Come, bitter conduct; come, unsavory guide! 116
Thou desperate pilot, now at once run on
The dashing rocks thy seasick weary bark!
Here's to my love! [*Drinks.*] O true apothecary! 119
Thy drugs are quick. Thus with a kiss I die. [*Falls.*

Enter Friar LAURENCE, *with lanthorn, crow, and spade.*

Friar. Saint Francis be my speed! how oft to-night
Have my old feet stumbled at graves! Who's there? 122
Balthasar. Here's one, a friend, and one that knows
     you well.
Friar. Bliss be upon you! Tell me, good my friend,
What torch is yond that vainly lends his light
To grubs and eyeless skulls? As I discern,
It burneth in the Capels' monument.
Balthasar. It doth so, holy sir; and there's my master,
One that you love.
Friar.   Who is it?
Balthasar.   Romeo.
Friar. How long hath he been there?
Balthasar.   Full half an hour.
Friar. Go with me to the vault.
Balthasar.   I dare not, sir.
My master knows not but I am gone hence,
And fearfully did menace me with death
If I did stay to look on his intents.
Friar. Stay then; I'll go alone. Fear comes upon me.
O, much I fear some ill unthrifty thing.   136
Balthasar. As I did sleep under this yew tree here,
I dreamt my master and another fought,   138
And that my master slew him.
Friar.   Romeo!
Alack, alack, what blood is this which stains
The stony entrance of this sepulchre?
What means these masterless and gory swords 142
To lie discolored by this place of peace?   143
                  [*Enters the tomb.*
Romeo! O, pale! Who else? What, Paris too?
And steeped in blood? Ah, what an unkind hour 145
Is guilty of this lamentable chance!
The lady stirs.   [JULIET *rises.*
Juliet. O comfortable friar! where is my lord? 148

101. "cousin": Tybalt would be his cousin (by marriage to Juliet).

103. "unsubstantial": without a material body.

111. "shake the yoke": the metaphor is one of a beast of burden coming home at the end of the day and shaking off his yoke.

115. "dateless": everlasting. "engrossing": seizing everything.

116. "conduct": conductor.

119. "true apothecary": Romeo can feel the poison overcoming him at once: he acknowledges that the apothecary has not misled him.

122. "stumbled": a sign of ill-omen.

136. "unthrifty": unlucky.

138. "I dreamt": does Balthasar really believe it to be a dream or does he put it like this to avoid admitting that he had defied his master's orders?

142. "masterless": abandoned.

143. "To lie": by lying. "discolored": by blood.

145. "unkind": unnatural.

148. "comfortable": giving comfort.

I do remember well where I should be,
And there I am. Where is my Romeo?
  Friar. I hear some noise. Lady, come from that nest
Of death, contagion, and unnatural sleep.
A greater power than we can contradict
Hath thwarted our intents. Come, come away.
Thy husband in thy bosom there lies dead;
And Paris too. Come, I'll dispose of thee
Among a sisterhood of holy nuns.
Stay not to question, for the watch is coming.
Come, go, good Juliet. I dare no longer stay.
  Juliet. Go, get thee hence, for I will not away.   160
             [*Exit* Friar.
What's here? A cup, closed in my true love's hand?
Poison, I see, hath been his timeless end.   162
O churl! drunk all, and left no friendly drop   163
To help me after? I will kiss thy lips.
Haply some poison yet doth hang on them
To make me die with a restorative.   [*Kisses him.*
Thy lips are warm!
  Chief Watchman. [*Within*] Lead, boy. Which way?
  Juliet. Yea, noise? Then I'll be brief. O happy
   dagger!   [*Snatches* ROMEO's *dagger.*
This is thy sheath! there rust, and let me die.
        [*She stabs herself and falls.*
     Enter PARIS' BOY *and* Watch.
  Boy. This is the place. There, where the torch doth
   burn.
  Chief Watchman. The ground is bloody. Search
   about the churchyard.
Go, some of you; whoe'er you find attach.   173
       [*Exeunt some of the* Watch.
Pitiful sight! here lies the County slain;
And Juliet bleeding, warm, and newly dead,
Who here hath lain this two days buried.
Go, tell the Prince; run to the Capulets;
Raise up the Montagues; some others search.
       [*Exeunt others of the* Watch.
We see the ground whereon these woes do lie,
But the true ground of all these piteous woes   180
We cannot without circumstance descry.   181
Enter some of the Watch, *with* ROMEO's Man BALTHASAR.
  Second Watchman. Here's Romeo's man. We found
   him in the churchyard.
  Chief Watchman. Hold him in safety till the Prince
   come hither.
    Enter FRIAR LAURENCE *and another* Watchman.
  Third Watchman. Here is a friar that trembles,
   sighs, and weeps.
We took this mattock and this spade from him
As he was coming from this churchyard side.
  Chief Watchman. A great suspicion! Stay the friar   187
   too.

    Enter the PRINCE *and* Attendants.

  Prince. What misadventure is so early up,   188
That calls our person from our morning rest?
     Enter CAPULET *and his* Wife *with others.*
  Capulet. What should it be, that is so shrieked
   abroad?
  Wife. O the people in the street cry 'Romeo,'

Juliet goes up to the body of her husband, and sees the cup in his clenched hand. He has drunk all the poison, churlishly leaving none for her, so she kisses his lips and, as the watch, led by the frightened page boy, approaches, she snatches Romeo's dagger and plunges it into her own heart, and dies, falling on Romeo's body.

The watch divides, some men to search the churchyard, others to remain below. They arrest the loyal Balthasar, and hold him in custody until the Prince comes.

---

160. "away": come away.

162. "timeless": untimely, and eternal.

163. "churl": this, of course, is said in a kindly way.

173. "attach": arrest, seize.

180. "ground of": reason for.

181. "circumstance": surrounding facts.

187. "Stay": keep in custody.

188. "up": going on.

ROMEO AND JULIET

ACT V SCENE III

Friar Laurence enters, trembling, sighing, and weeping, and they "attach" him, too. The senior Capulets enter, followed by the Prince. Three violent deaths have to be accounted for: Paris', Romeo's, and—as it now strangely appears—Juliet's.

Lord Montague enters, and before the Prince points out his dead son and former heir, the old nobleman relates that his wife has died, that same evening, of grief on hearing of her son's exile. On seeing the body of his Romeo, he feebly asks "what further woe conspires" against his age. The Prince asks them all to "seal up the mouth of outrage for a while" until all the doubts, or "ambiguities," have been cleared up.

Friar Laurence then explains how these tragic events came to take place. The Prince listens to the friar's account, examines the circumstantial evidence, exonerates both the friar and Balthasar, and calls out to Capulet and Montague, showing them how everybody has been punished as a result of their enmity. Even the Prince has "lost a brace of kinsmen" (Mercutio and Paris). He talks aristocratically of these kinsmen, almost as if they had been a brace of grouse, as befits a great Duke.

Some 'Juliet,' and some 'Paris'; and all run,
With open outcry, toward our monument. 193
   Prince. What fear is this which startles in your ears? 194
   Chief Watchman. Sovereign, here lies the County
     Paris slain;
And Romeo dead; and Juliet, dead before,
Warm and new killed.
   Prince. Search, seek, and know how this foul murder comes.
   Chief Watchman. Here is a friar, and slaughtered
     Romeo's man,
With instruments upon them fit to open
These dead men's tombs.
   Capulet. O heavens! O wife, look how our daughter
     bleeds!
This dagger hath mista'en, for, lo, his house 203
Is empty on the back of Montague, 204
And it missheathed in my daughter's bosom!
   Wife. O me! this sight of death is as a bell
That warns my old age to a sepulchre. 207

        Enter MONTAGUE *and others*.

   Prince. Come, Montague; for thou art early up
To see thy son and heir more early down. 209
   Montague. Alas, my liege, my wife is dead to-night!
Grief of my son's exile hath stopped her breath.
What further woe conspires against mine age?
   Prince. Look, and thou shalt see.
   Montague. O thou untaught! what manners is in this, 214
To press before thy father to a grave? 215
   Prince. Seal up the mouth of outrage for a while, 216
Till we can clear these ambiguities
And know their spring, their head, their true descent; 218
And then will I be general of your woes 219
And lead you even to death. Meantime forbear,
And let mischance be slave to patience. 221
Bring forth the parties of suspicion. 222
   Friar. I am the greatest, able to do least, 223
Yet most suspected, as the time and place
Doth make against me, of this direful murder; 225
And here I stand, both to impeach and purge 226
Myself condemned and myself excused.
   Prince. Then say at once what thou dost know in
     this.
   Friar. I will be brief, for my short date of breath 229
Is not so long as is a tedious tale.
Romeo, there dead, was husband to that Juliet;
And she, there dead, that Romeo's faithful wife.
I married them; and their stol'n marriage day 233
Was Tybalt's doomsday, whose untimely death
Banished the new-made bridegroom from this city;
For whom, and not for Tybalt, Juliet pined.
You, to remove that siege of grief from her, 237
Betrothed and would have married her perforce
To County Paris. Then comes she to me
And with wild looks bid me devise some mean
To rid her from this second marriage,
Or in my cell there would she kill herself.
Then gave I her (so tutored by my art)
A sleeping potion; which so took effect
As I intended, for it wrought on her

193. "With open outcry": a metaphor from hunting, when the dogs are "in full cry" after the game.

194. "startles in": alarms, shocks.

203. "mista'en": gone to the wrong place.
"his house": its sheath (personified, to augment the heinousness of the deed of which it was the instrument).

204. "Montague": Romeo.

207. "warns": summons.

209. "down": dead.

214. "O thou untaught!": unmannerly, ignorant person!

215. "To press . . . grave?": as if he were pushing through a doorway in front of his father.

216. "outrage": passion.

218. "spring . . . head . . . descent": metaphors from a stream flowing down from its source, standing for the beginning and the sequence of "these ambiguities."

219-20. "general . . . death": at the head of your woes (to get vengeance or at least inflict punishment) even if it leads to the death of those responsible.

221. "mischance be slave to patience": disaster be ruled by patience.

222. "parties of suspicion": suspects.

223. "the greatest": suspected most.

225. "doth make": do inform, witness.

226-7. "both . . . excused": the friar acknowledges that he can be accused of being the cause of these deaths (his condemnation), but not that it was his intention (that is his excuse).

229. "date of breath": time I have to live.

223. "stol'n": secret.

237. "siege": cause (or, which besieged her).

ROMEO AND JULIET

ACT V SCENE III

The catastrophe is redeemed by the reconciliation of the houses of Capulet and Montague, and it is Capulet who first steps forward to seize Montague's hand as that of a brother, in token of his daughter's "jointure" i.e., her union with Romeo.

The Prince says "the sun, for sorrow, will not show his head"—a fine piece of pathetic fallacy expressing the shame of nature at the manners of men.

The dramatic purposes served by this scene are:

1. It provides the solution of the plot, or the denouement of the entire play.

2. It brings about four deaths.

3. It brings all the other participants—except the nurse—on stage for the final curtain calls.

4. It is a melodramatic, terrifying, ghastly, horrific, and picturesque scene.

5. It contains the moral, or postscript.

6. It contains a concise resume, in Friar Laurence's terminal speech, of all of the events leading up to the catastrophic resolution.

7. It provides 'catharsis' or emotional purification and relief, according to the Aristotelian criteria of tragedy.

The form of death. Meantime I writ to Romeo	246
That he should hither come as this dire night	247
To help to take her from her borrowed grave,	
Being the time the potion's force should cease.	
But he which bore my letter, Friar John,	
Was stayed by accident, and yesternight	
Returned my letter back. Then all alone	
At the prefixed hour of her waking	
Came I to take her from her kindred's vault;	
Meaning to keep her closely at my cell	255
Till I conveniently could send to Romeo.	
But when I came, some minute ere the time	
Of her awakening, here untimely lay	
The noble Paris and true Romeo dead.	
She wakes; and I entreated her come forth	260
And bear this work of heaven with patience;	261
But then a noise did scare me from the tomb,	
And she, too desperate, would not go with me,	
But, as it seems, did violence on herself.	
All this I know, and to the marriage	
Her nurse is privy; and if aught in this	
Miscarried by my fault, let my old life	
Be sacrificed, some hour before his time,	268
Unto the rigor of severest law.	
Prince. We still have known thee for a holy man.	270
Where's Romeo's man? What can he say in this?	
Balthasar. I brought my master news of Juliet's death;	
And then in post he came from Mantua	273
To this same place, to this same monument.	
This letter he early bid me give his father,	275
And threat'ned me with death, going in the vault,	276
If I departed not and left him there.	
Prince. Give me the letter. I will look on it.	
Where is the County's page that raised the watch?	279
Sirrah, what made your master in this place?	280
Boy. He came with flowers to strew his lady's grave;	
And bid me stand aloof, and so I did.	
Anon comes one with light to ope the tomb;	
And by and by my master drew on him;	284
And then I ran away to call the watch.	
Prince. This letter doth make good the friar's words,	
Their course of love, the tidings of her death;	
And here he writes that he did buy a poison	
Of a poor pothecary, and therewithal	
Came to this vault to die, and lie with Juliet.	
Where be these enemies? Capulet, Montague,	
See what a scourge is laid upon your hate,	
That heaven finds means to kill your joys with love.	
And I, for winking at your discords too,	294
Have lost a brace of kinsmen. All are punished.	295
Capulet. O brother Montague, give me thy hand	
This is my daughter's jointure, for no more	297
Can I demand.	
Montague. But I can give thee more;	
For I will raise her statue in pure gold,	
That whiles Verona by that name is known,	
There shall no figure at such rate beset	301
As that of true and faithful Juliet.	

246. "form": appearance.

247. "as": on.

255. "closely": secretly.

260. "She wakes": notice this dramatic transition to the present tense, making the effect more crisp and forceful. The effect is similar (but in reverse order of time) to that of l. 87, where Romeo calls himself "a dead man."

261. "this work of heaven": Romeo's death.

268. "his": its.

270. "still": always.

273. "in post": post haste.

275. "early": i.e., in the morning.

276. "going": as he was going.

279. "raised": sent for, called, summoned.

280. "made": was doing.

284. "by and by": at once. "your joys": your children.

294. "winking at": closing my eyes to.

295. "a brace of kinsmen": Mercutio and Paris.

297. "jointure": that which the bridegroom or his parents settle on the bride.

301. "at such rate to be set": be valued this high.

Capulet. As rich shall Romeo's by his lady lie—
Poor sacrifices of our enmity!   304
  Prince. A glooming peace this morning with it 305
    brings
  The sun for sorrow will not show his head.
Go hence, to have more talk of these sad things;
  Some shall be pardoned, and some punished;
For never was a story of more woe
Than this of Juliet and her Romeo. [*Exeunt omnes.*

304. "sacrifices of our enmity": offerings of our hatred (which has now ceased).

305. "glooming": melancholy.

Bibliography

EDITIONS

A New Variorum Edition of Shakespeare, ed. Horace H. Furness. New York: J. B. Lippincott, 1871-1919. (Reprints by The American Scholar and Dover Publications.) Each play is dealt with in a separate volume of monumental scholarship.

The Yale Shakespeare, ed. Helge Kökeritz and Charles T. Prouty. New Haven: Yale University Press, 1955——. A multi-volume edition founded on modern scholarship.

COMMENTARY AND CRITICISM

Bentley, G. E. *Shakespeare and His Theatre.* Lincoln: University of Nebraska Press, 1964 (paperback). Illuminating discussion of the actual conditions under which, and for which, Shakespeare wrote.

Bradley, A. C. *Shakespearean Tragedy: Lectures on Hamlet, Othello, King Lear, Macbeth.* New York: Macmillan, 1904. (Paperback ed.; New York: Meridian Books, 1955.) A classic examination of the great tragedies.

Chambers, Edmund K. *William Shakespeare: A Study of Facts and Problems,* 2 vols. Oxford: Clarendon Press, 1930. Indispensable source for bibliographical and historical information.

Chute, Marchette. *Shakespeare of London.* New York: E. P. Dutton, 1949. A vivid account of Shakespeare's career in the dynamic Elizabethan metropolis.

Granville-Barker, Harley. *Prefaces to Shakespeare.* London: Sidgwick & Jackson, 1927-47. (2 vols.; Princeton: Princeton University Press, 1947.) Stimulating studies of ten plays by a scholarly man of the theater.

Harbage, Alfred. *Shakespeare's Audience.* New York: Columbia University Press, 1941. Revealing approach to Shakespeare as a practical man of the theater.

Knight, Wilson. *The Wheel of Fire.* London: Oxford University Press, 1930. Stresses the power of intuition to capture the total poetic experience of Shakespeare's work.

Spurgeon, Caroline. *Shakespeare's Imagery and What It Tells Us.* Cambridge: Cambridge University Press, 1935. A psychological study of the playwright's imagery as a means to understanding the man himself.